OBSTACLES PRESS

By Chris Brady and Orrin Woodward

Second Edition, June 2013

Published by:

Obstaclés Press
4072 Market Place Dr., Flint, MI 48507

Photography by Chris Brady
"Destiny Restored from Above" poem by Orrin Woodward
All other poems by Chris Brady

Cover and layout designed by Norm Williams, nwa-inc.com

lifeleadership.com

Printed in the United States of America

To those who would dare live an excellent life.

"Life is the art of drawing without an eraser."
– John Christian

"Before you can win the fight, you've got to be in the fight."
– Bill Walsh

ACKNOWLEDGEMENTS

Writing a book is an odd endeavor, one that involves long moments of study, thought, and wrangling with language. However, the image of the lone sage hunched over a desk, with pen and quill in hand, is only a partial truth. The real story involves much more of a team effort than the casual reader may realize.

In the production of this work, as with all our previous ones, we are deeply indebted to many individuals whose contribution and expertise were critical to its completion. First and foremost we would like to thank our wives and children for their undying love and support, and on many occasions, patience. It cannot be easy to watch two crazy men get caught up in their collective imagination like a small cyclone, to the detriment of all other responsibilities and considerations. We thank you for allowing us the freedom to create.

We are also heartily grateful for both the friendship and the leadership of Rob Hallstrand, who has proven to be world class at running the organizational side of our lives. We would also like to thank the entire staff of Obstaclés Press, and particularly Bill Rousseau, for long hours and tireless efforts behind the scenes. Our graphic artist, Norm Williams, also deserves a very special thank you for carrying the heavy load a graphical book like this requires. His creativity and expertise are certainly one of the main characters in this book!

As always, our very lives and every aspect of them are the precious gift of our Lord and Savior, Jesus Christ. To Him be the honor and the glory.

INTRODUCTION

After yet another round of cancer surgery Donald Hall wrote, "For weeks after my last operation – frail and without energy, sleeping ten hours – I looked in my house at all the books I had not read and wept for my inability to read them. Or I looked at great books I had read too quickly in my avidity – telling myself I would return to them later. There is never a *later*, but for most of my life I have believed in later." Life is short. Life is precious. The older we get, the more we can relate to Hall's comments. Life is something we feel deep down inside to be special, to be treasured, to be handled correctly.

John Gardner wrote, "The society which scorns excellence in plumbing because plumbing is a humble activity, and tolerates shoddiness in philosophy because it is an exalted activity, will have neither good plumbing nor good philosophy. Neither its pipes nor its theories will hold water."

Frank Capra, the director of the classic film *It's a Wonderful Life*, was asked about the central message of his movie. After thinking a few moments, Capra responded, "I believe the real message of *It's a Wonderful Life* is this: that under the sun, nothing is insignificant to God."

In these three abstract considerations we can get a picture of the components of a life well lived. We see that a moment wasted is lost forever, and so somehow life is to be lived in the moment, but also still lived out in an excellent way, because not even a split second of it is insignificant to God. In other words, life counts. We count. And the way we live our lives counts. To squander our time is the easiest temptation, but it results in the greatest of regrets, and perhaps the greatest tragedy.

"Life is short." "Life is precious." "Life is fleeting." "Life is good." "It's your life." "Choose life." "Life in the fast lane." "The high life." "It's my life." There seems to be no limit to the phrases and platitudes attempting to express something about this mystery called life. Then, among other things, there is *Life* cereal, *Life* magazine, and *Life* the game, demonstrating the preponderance of commercial applications of the concept. Life is in our thoughts, in our commercial products, in our language, and in our discourse. We all know what it is. We all have our own to experience.

Yet at the same time we know so little about it. God's power to create life, to bless our lives, and to give us everlasting life is beyond our total comprehension. We each have experience with life because we are each alive, but that fact is far from qualifying us as experts of the topic.

Nope. Life is predominantly a profound mystery: a voyage of discovery, a pilgrimage to a higher purpose, a test, a gift, a game. Again, we can barely talk about the subject without giving way to a rush of metaphors.

In the pages that follow are varied commentaries covering several aspects of this many-faceted and fascinating subject. We call them the "8 Fs." These are: Faith, Family, Friendship, Fun, Freedom, Fitness, Finances, and Following. There could certainly be more (readers have offered up Fishing, Football, Food, Fashion, and Firearms, among others), but we feel the enormity of the subject can be adequately surveyed from the vantage point of these eight critical positions. In our minds they comprise the spokes of a wheel, with life being the hub and our interaction with others and the outside world being the rim.

We also like to look at the word, "life" as an acronym: Living Intentionally For Excellence. It is in this way we seek to maximize our gifts in each of the eight categories and utilize them in a purpose that transcends ourselves and our selfish interests. A life well lived is one deployed for a higher purpose, calling, and being. The converse is a wasted life, one in which our blessings are squandered primarily on personal peace and affluence. In such a life, boredom is quite possibly the embarrassment we feel when we know we could be doing more with our gifts. Living a life of excellence does not happen accidentally, but rather through significant effort expended thoughtfully and intentionally – that is the subject of this book.

Herein the reader will not find a pedantic organization of material, as if the topic could be so tidily arranged. Instead, what follows is a smorgasbord of nourishment for each of the eight areas. The arrangement is a bit scrambled, but not to worry, so is the format of the material itself. There are short and long commentaries, as well as 580 of the authors' most popular and poignant "one-liner" quotes (as first made public to their respective followers on Twitter). This seemingly haphazard arrangement is intentionally designed to enhance readability, retention, and enjoyment. We can only hope that through graphical representations and creative arrangements we have hit our mark. We leave it up to the reader to decide.

Though this book is couched in fun art and bright colors, do not rush past the main point: Your life counts; it is significant; and it matters. You have been given marvelous and unique gifts, and you have been given them for a purpose. Resist the disease of modern Western living, in which comfort and materialism permeate daily existence. Instead, intentionally choose to rise above your times and live an uncommon life.

It has been said that our life is a gift from God, while what we do with it is our gift back to Him. In view of this, it may be your life, but it's not yours to waste.

66NO ONE SHOULD EVER GO HUNGRY, WHAT WITH CHEWING OURSELVES OUT, EATING CROW AND SWALLOWING PRIDE.**99**

66TO THINK THAT THE WISE ARE NOT CAPABLE OF FOLLY IS NOT WISE.**99**

"The limiting factor on your success is not the size of the obstacles, but the size of your dream."

"People forget what you kept, but they will never forget what you gave."

66CYNICISM IS WHAT HAPPENS WHEN SKEPTICISM IS GIVEN TOO MUCH LATITUDE.**99**

66NO GUTS, NO STORY.**99**

66NEVER UNDERESTIMATE THE DANGER OF UNDERESTIMATING.**99**

"Life is too short to be little."

"The only substitute for good manners is fast reflexes."

"There are no dead ends in life, only dead end thinking."

"Thinking is the toughest kind of work which is why so many people avoid it."

"If we're going to make mistakes anyway, we might as well learn from them – 'teachable moments.'"

"If you fill your head with positive thoughts, there won't be any room left for negative ones."

WHAT WE HAVE AND WHAT WE ARE GIVEN ARE NOT AS IMPORTANT AS WHAT WE CONTRIBUTE AND WHAT WE LEAVE BEHIND.

I AM REALLY STARTING TO THINK IGNORANCE IS MORE DANGEROUS THAN PLAIN OLD EVIL.

"Absolute power doesn't corrupt, but rather, reveals character."

"Don't mistake thinking for action & don't mistake action for results."

SOMETIMES THE LEADER IS THE LEADER BECAUSE HE IS THE ONLY ONE SURE HE DOESN'T HAVE ALL THE ANSWERS.

WHEN PEOPLE DEMAND THE GOVERNMENT 'DO SOMETHING,' THE 'DOING' USUALLY COMES AT THE EXPENSE OF FREEDOM.

He Who Laughs, Lasts

Leadership is about the influence one has with others. To gain that influence, one must be trustworthy and at the same time be an effective performer, visionary, and a host of other things we described in our book *Launching a Leadership Revolution*. There are some "soft" side considerations, too. One of these, often ignored, is humor.

Both the ability to inspire mirth and the quickness with which one laughs are effective skills in gaining influence. Why? Because people like to be around those who are fun and make them laugh.

Below are ten ways to increase your ability to both appreciate humor and to contribute to the laughter:

DON'T TAKE YOURSELF TOO SERIOUSLY

1. Don't take yourself too seriously. The world is overstuffed with people puffed up with their own self-importance. Distance yourselves from these bores by taking everything seriously except yourself.
2. Have an attitude of gratitude. One of the things holding many people back from humor is their bad attitude. They are in too bad of a mood to see the funny side of anything. You won't appreciate the subtlety that is humor unless you are appreciative to begin with.
3. Make your foibles the subject matter. The most enjoyable people to be around are those who are able and quick to laugh at themselves. Conversely, the worst kind of people to be around are those who laugh at others.
4. Stay away from sarcasm. Humor is dangerous, especially when it is biting or berating. Tread carefully – especially when it comes to your "humor style." Sarcasm may be fun to dish out, but it is never enjoyable to receive.

> When people intrinsically feel that you mean no harm and are instead only interested in their well being, they will be unguarded around you and open to your every statement.

> The most enjoyable people to be around are those who are able and quick to laugh at themselves.

5. Be good-hearted. One of the things most endearing about someone is their good heart. It comes through in everything they say. When people intrinsically feel that you mean no harm and are instead only interested in their well being, they will be unguarded around you and open to your every statement. This relaxed posture makes everything you say more funny.

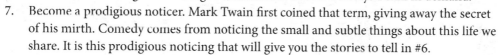

6. Tell stories. Some of the merriest moments occur naturally as we live our lives. Capture those moments in your mind in story form and save them for later. Being able to tell good, humorous stories is always a skill in demand.

7. Become a prodigious noticer. Mark Twain first coined that term, giving away the secret of his mirth. Comedy comes from noticing the small and subtle things about this life we share. It is this prodigious noticing that will give you the stories to tell in #6.

8. Implement techniques. There are some skills that enhance humor, such as timing, delivery, facial expressions, dramatization, gestures, and the like. Over time and with practice, develop your own style.

9. Be circular. Bringing something back around into a conversation that occurred earlier can be hilarious. Watch for ways to apply earlier humor to new situations.

10. Be a good laugher. One of the keys to reducing tension in a room is to be a good laugher yourself. Laughter is actually contagious. Be quick to enjoy others and their stabs at humor and their own moods will lighten and be more prepared to receive your quips as well.

We could go on all day here, but one final piece of advice about humor: know when to quit!

Comedy comes from noticing the small and subtle things about this life we share.

The World Needs Leaders

Perhaps now as much as ever, the world is in dire need of leadership. I don't speak of the candy-coated, teleprompter variety, or the plastic-faced tell-you-what-you-want-to-hear politician. I am also not referring to the high-born, or the well-connected, or the well-to-do. I don't refer to the do-gooders, or the world-controllers, neither the people arrogant enough to think they can save the world if only they could impose enough of their infallible wisdom upon others.

No. What I'm referring to is real leadership: the kind that bubbles up from among the population of good, hard-working, honest people. I don't know why, but it seems as if the general mindset of people today runs along the tracks of, "There ought to be a law," or "The government should do something," or "An agency must be created to make this better." This mindset is dangerous, cowardly, and lazy. The world has rarely been made better by centralized, top-down impositions of somebody's concept of utopia, and yet, that is the exact type of solution to which we have either become accustomed, or conditioned.

Many, many of our problems today are the direct result of top-down, collectivized, centralized decision-making. It's "Government this," "agency that," until we are smothered under regulation and control. The same false thinking that created them cannot solve the problems thus created.

The challenges of our times call for solutions, for certain, but solutions of the grass-roots variety; fixes that spring from the individuals most affected, and most concerned, with the state of things in their world. Individual initiative and pluck, combined with ingenuity and creativity, is responsible for more good and progress in the world than any collective body of government bureaucrats and professional nincompoops. This occurs when individuals are free to conceive and create, build and construct, produce and prosper. In short, when individuals lead.

> Leadership is not a subset of management theory or political theory or business theory. It is central to all human activity.

Leadership is not a subset of management theory or political theory or business theory. It is central to all human activity. There are always those individuals who dare to stand up to injustice, stand in the gap of need, and stand on principle. They use what they have, where they are, to fix what they see as being wrong. They improve things, move them along, and contribute to the overall picture by their individual actions.

That is leadership.

And we need it now from individuals everywhere.

Will you respond?

"Leaders do what ought to be done whether their deeds are known by thousands or known by no one."

"Ideas have enormous consequences in a person's life because you ultimately become what you believe."

YOUR SHORT TERM DESIRES ARE THE ENEMIES OF YOUR LONG-TERM DREAMS.

SUCCESS IS ELUSIVE TO MOST PEOPLE BECAUSE THEY TRY TO SPREAD IT OUT OVER TOO MANY ENDEAVORS.

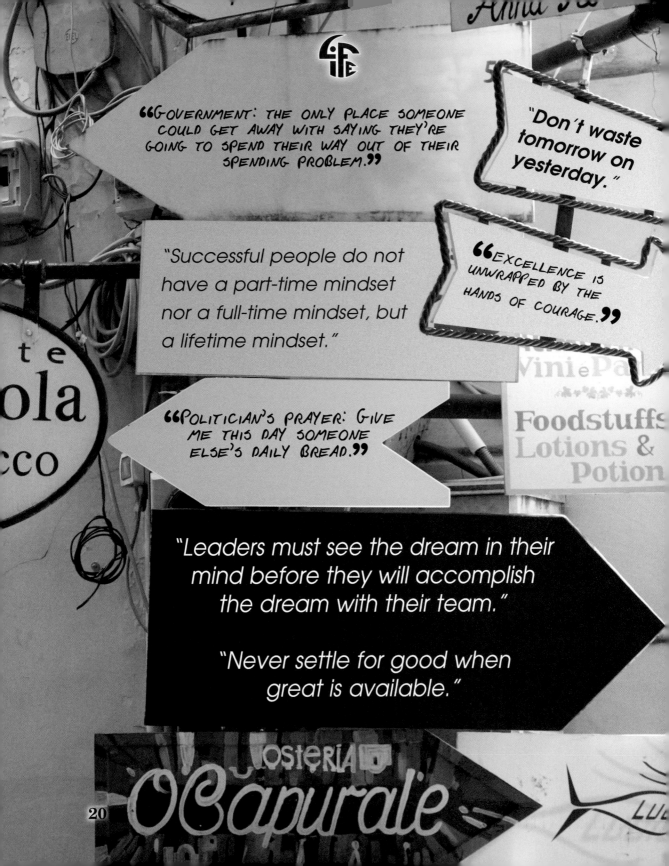

"Government: the only place someone could get away with saying they're going to spend their way out of their spending problem."

"Don't waste tomorrow on yesterday."

"Successful people do not have a part-time mindset nor a full-time mindset, but a lifetime mindset."

"Excellence is unwrapped by the hands of courage."

"Politician's prayer: Give me this day someone else's daily bread."

"Leaders must see the dream in their mind before they will accomplish the dream with their team."

"Never settle for good when great is available."

20

Pleasure, Pain, and Purpose

We strive mightily to make things perfect. But would we really like them that way? What would a game of golf be like if every drive and putt were perfect every time? What would be the fun in hunting if every outing produced record game with perfect shots? Would victory of any kind carry reward if it didn't lie on the other side of struggle? Who would want to see a movie with no conflict to be resolved?

As we deal with the difficulties of this world, it may be good to consider that while we do not like pain, pleasure is not that much better for us. Ponder this: too much struggle and heartache drives us to despair. But on the other hand, too much pleasure and freedom produces boredom and emptiness. (Think of the many famous people who apparently "had it all" but destroyed their lives.)

Could it be that we are only "happy," nay, sane, living somewhere in between? Before we rail too hard against struggle as an enemy, perhaps we should make ourselves equally aware of his counterpart at the opposite end. At least pain and suffering are obviously hurtful. Pleasure and ease are sneak-attackers.

So what are we to do in between?

I posit that living life on purpose, for a purpose, is the way we are supposed to navigate these waters. We will suffer some pain, experience some pleasures, tossed about by both as on waves, but our vessel should be pointed at that distant shore. It matters where we are sailing, and it matters how we sail. As you set your compass, I recommend Ecclesiastes 12:13 for a bearing: "Let us hear the conclusion of the whole matter: Fear God, and keep His commandments: for this is the whole duty of man."

> Too much struggle and heartache drives us to despair.

> "Ingratitude produces pride while gratitude produces humility."

> "In life, most people surrender what is possible for what is comfortable."

LIVING WITH SPECIFIC INTENT

Early in our business journey, while attending a leadership seminar, a speaker said five words we have never forgotten: "Do everything with specific intent." It may seem strange to some how five words can have such a profound effect, changing the way we viewed life from that day forward; but personal development seminars improve one's results by consistently improving perspective, and that's exactly what occurred that day. We learned productivity is not the same as being busy. **In the game of life it's easy to stay busy, but it requires focus to have specific intents.**

What are the key areas upon which to focus in order to make leaders productive and not just busy? Socrates said, "The unexamined life is not worth living." In order to improve our impact we must examine life, searching for which areas are not measuring up to our expectations, all the while asking: are we doing everything with specific intent? This powerful concept changes lives when applied consistently. As a community, we have identified eight "F's" that can make a difference in someone's life, as

> *The unexamined life is not worth living.*
> – Socrates

stated in this book's "Introduction," these are: **Faith, Family, Fitness, Finances, Freedom, Friends, Fun, and Following.** Study this list and ponder which areas, if improved, would make the biggest impact in the quality of your life. For example, let's say Family, Finances, and Fitness, are the three areas in which you would like to improve. The next step would be to develop a specific intent in each area, game planning for success.

Let's assume you're married and have several children. It's easy to wander through marriage and child rearing with no specific intent. When issues arise they are handled, but issues consistently and persistently pop up, leaving you bewildered. This happens when there is no overarching plan or no specific intent, just day-by-day living – but it doesn't have to be that way. One of the greatest benefits of associating with a community of learners is the realization that everyone there is also working to improve in some or all of the "8 F" categories. In the community of LIFE it's not only acceptable to borrow knowledge from your neighbor's experiences, it's encouraged. Life is so busy, hectic, and challenging that no one has the time, let alone the inclination, to gather all the answers for themselves through the timely process of trial and error, or the nearly as difficult approach of researching all the available resources. However, *all* of us together are stronger than *any* of us apart. What if another leader, one that you trusted and respected, who successfully raised four children, provided you with his

or her secrets to success? Wouldn't this speed up the learning process for you? Isn't that a great start (and in fact, a shortcut) on developing a specific intent game plan? By listening to the LIFE audio materials, reading books on the roles and responsibilities of each spouse, and studying the principles of top parents, one can make major headway in a short amount of time. Why head into such an important responsibility without all the help that you can get? As Isaac Newton said when receiving an award, "If I have seen further, it's because I have stood on the shoulders of giants." **Stand on the shoulders of giants** who have accomplished what you desire, and use the expertise of others to develop specific intent for your family.

What about the area of finances? In the typical family, less than a month of income separates them from insolvency. Living so close to the brink of disaster is stressful and not recommended. In fact, it's so stressful it makes one wonder why so many people live this way in the first place. The answer is often the simple truth that no one has taught them the financial principles that, if applied consistently, would produce the desired results. Most people who make $30,000 per year believe if they made $40,000 per year their troubles would be over. Strangely, though, people who make $40,000 per year seem to believe it would take $50,000 a year to solve *their* problems. The trouble with this thinking is that no matter how much you make, if you spend it all, you're constantly at the financial cliff. In other words, it's not what you make but what you keep that determines financial success. People can be financially solid making $30,000 per year. On the other hand, people can be financially insolvent making $500,000 per year. We have witnessed people in both positions numerous times over the years. Until the orgy of spending is arrested, the financial struggles will continue, and often times get worse. The good news is that thousands of people have applied the financial laws taught in the LIFE materials and have taken control of their financial futures. Many people, who were a mess financially, now enjoy debt-free lifestyles because they learned to apply the financial laws of success in their lives. If you're tired of living paycheck to paycheck, if you're tired of staring into the financial abyss, then get a checkup from the neck up by learning financial literacy. It's time to develop specific intent and master the financial laws of success.

Finally, let's discuss fitness. North America is greatly suffering from a lack of fitness. From poor eating habits, high stress, and lack of exercise, bad health is debilitating many – but it doesn't have to be that way. Thousands of people, applying good and proper health and fitness habits, have developed healthier life choices and are now enjoying the benefits of better information. Most North Americans, by simply eating better, could shed ten to fifteen pounds and almost immediately feel better physically *and* mentally. Few people realize that eating right is over 80% of the challenge in improving one's health. A steady diet of garbage food will lead to a garbage body. Furthermore, compound poor eating with high stress, and one has a recipe for strokes, heart attacks, cancer and more. Fitness cannot make up for genetics, but many times it can make the difference between healthy lifestyles and recurring sicknesses. Since we only have one body, doesn't it make sense to treat it right? One of our best friends was, according to his doctor, a walking stroke, waiting to happen. The doctor even forbid our friend from doing any strenuous exercise until he could get his blood pressure back under control. We are happy to report that, through the fitness information available through the LIFE community, his blood pressure is now below average, and through a regimen of healthy eating, healthy supplementation, and exercise, he has lost thirty pounds and feels better than he has in decades. This is just one of many examples. Fitness is another very important area upon which to focus with specific intent.

Awsome explains you

So study the "8Fs" for yourself. In which of the areas do you need to improve, but haven't yet applied the proper leverage to get the job done? By having a supporting community with you, the work is easier, the information more readily available, the tasks more enjoyable, and the victory much sweeter. It is time to overcome whatever Goliath has been holding you back. Instead of circling your Goliath and

looking for a weak spot in his armor, arm yourself with better weapons of information and involvement in a community. Step out of the crowd, beat Goliath, and claim your victory.

We are reminded of the story of Sir Edmund Hillary, the man who made several failed attempts at climbing Mt. Everest before eventually succeeding. After yet another of his abortive attempts he attended a meeting with his partners and supporters to determine whether they should try again. Many felt it was hopeless and thought they should give up. Finally, Hillary stood up from the table, walked over to the wall where a picture of Mt. Everest hung, and shook his fist furiously at the picture, exclaiming, "Mt. Everest, I WILL conquer you because you cannot get any bigger than you already are, but I continue to grow each day." In the same way your own personal Goliath isn't getting any bigger, either, but *you* can get bigger. You will beat him by getting bigger, stronger, and better. Remember: your past failures have no power to block your future victories – unless you let them. It all boils down to choices. Instead of creating a life of regrets by avoiding the challenges necessary to accomplish our dreams, why not create a life of dreams by avoiding your regrets? As Helen Keller said, "Life is a daring bold adventure, or it's nothing at all." We say, **"Life should be lived with specific intent, or it's not lived at all."**

Puffy Faces

Struggles and obstacles are a normal part of high achievement. Inertia, laziness, and complacency must be violently beaten back with the blunt sword of determination. Excellence only comes with a price, and sometimes paying that price will almost bring us to our knees. This kind of talk is nothing new to high-achievers. They know the miles they've traveled and the resistance they've had to overcome. They understand that nothing great can be accomplished without a heroic struggle, often the long and drudging kind of struggle, requiring daily fortitude in the quiet, unseen moments that separate the best from the rest.

Many people, it seems, are not prepared for this. They dream of the lofty prizes, get starry-eyed at the glitter of success, but become bogged down along the journey. Uninitiated into the corps of the courageous, they don't always know how to respond. This is when the "Puffy Face" symptom sets in.

Perhaps you've seen it. The Puffy Face, that is. It's a condition that afflicts some people once they realize greatness will exact a price from them. Their eyes don't light up quite like before. Their step is no longer quick and light. Their smile is forced and wooden. But most of all, their entire countenance seems to bloat with self-absorbed doubt, as if all the unfairness in the world has assembled within their cheeks and chin.

"This is hard," their fat jowls seem to say, or "I'm not sure this is worth it," or "The grass is greener somewhere else, surely," or, "If God would have wanted me to succeed at this, He'd have made it easier!" or "Success can't be this hard for everybody else, something is unfairly stacked up against me!" And of course, with each passing excuse, the face puffs up even more.

Puffy Face is a quitter's disease. Avoid it at all costs. It is very hard to reduce the swelling and regain the countenance of a determined warrior, but it can be done. A return to the heroic will involve several antidotes, including reconnecting with one's purpose, refreshing one's dream, and counting one's blessings. The challenge seems to be that once a victim is afflicted with the Puffy Face, he or she is unwilling or uninterested in taking these remedies. Sadly, most Puffy Faces simply fade away into oblivion, blaming others as they go. They will never achieve anything of significance, taking their personal limitations and failures with them into the next endeavor, which, inevitably, will only eventuate in another Puffy Face episode, at which point the cycle starts over again!

It would be much better to muster the courage to beat back the Puffy Face and push through the tough moments. The victory podium is worth it, and to be sure, there are no Puffy Faces there!

> *It would be much better to muster the courage to beat back the Puffy Face and push through the tough moments.*

66 EXPERIENCE IS NOT WHAT HAPPENS TO YOU, BUT WHAT YOU HAPPEN TO DO WITH WHAT HAPPENS TO YOU. 99

66 THE CRITIC HATES THE MOST THAT WHICH HE WAS TOO CHICKEN TO DO HIMSELF. 99

"Many times in life, those who do the most correcting, need the most correcting."

"People are the same in a lot of different ways; and they are different in a lot of the same ways."

"Losing is good sometimes: it makes you appreciate winning all that much more."

"Leaders are givers and takers: givers of credit and takers of responsibility and blame."

BLU PORTER

POSITANO

complain about what you permit to be."

"Excuses are used to justify leaving the scene of truth without changing."

"Avoidance of self deception is a matter of integrity not comfort."

"Always carry a salt shaker; the time is surely coming when you'll have to eat some crow."

"I would rather face my fears than lose, but most people would rather lose than face their fears."

"Leaders know that the fruit of life is out on a limb."

"Winners make every setback a floor to launch higher. Non-winners make every setback a ceiling to launch lower."

"Most people settle in life with no satisfaction. Winners are satisfied without ever settling."

"Leadership is an art that comes from the heart."

"Listening is an action sport for leaders."

Self-Deception and Leadership Results

Results in life are inversely proportional to the level of self-deception. I know that statement can sound harsh, but hardly anything amazes me more than the self-deception levels obtained by people. In a desire to protect their fragile egos, potentially successful people would rather destroy their results than confront the facts. If things are going poorly, the first step is to confront the facts. Most people when they read this are quick to say, "Yes, I confronted the facts and it is everyone's fault but my own." The only problem with this answer is that if everyone else is to blame, then how can you change to get better? Yes, bad teammates can hurt you, but they cannot stop you as only you can choose to quit your leadership journey. Let's walk through a couple of key points to keep you from self-deception.

FIRST, ALWAYS LOOK AT THE DATA

If the data is not available then you must design a reporting mechanism to get the data. Anything that plans on succeeding must have a scoreboard. How do you score points? How do you know if you are winning or losing if no one is keeping score? I know this sounds basic, but the number of times I have studied business issues to find out the alleged leader was not keeping score is legion! Can you imagine going to a football game where there was no scoreboard? Every team would claim they were the best and demand pay increases plus signing bonuses, if there wasn't a scoreboard to keep them from their delusionary thinking. I love the statement, "In God we trust; all others must have data." You claim to be a great leader? Back it up by your results. If you have no results, then you are the proverbial king with no clothes on, suffering from self-deception.

Second, no matter how bad the facts are, there is always the potential for a turnaround as long as you do not blame others and/or deceive yourself. I have never seen a hopeless situation, but have seen many hopeless leaders in situations. I believe one of the strongest attributes of any leader is his undying optimism to get through no matter what the odds against him. By accurately confronting the data, it will force you to assign blame to yourself and generate action plans to get better. Only people who assess the facts as they actually are and develop game plans to improve will reach their potential for excellence and have followers. Self-deception is an immediate cancellation of the growth process and must be avoided at all cost. **Anyone claiming to be a leader should be judged by his scoreboard and not by his self-proclamations.**

Third, choose to be a producer, not an exploiter. I love the Texas saying, "Big hat and no cattle." No matter how big the hat you wear, if you have no cattle, you have no results. The Internet Age has allowed people with little or no results to make beautiful websites, exciting videos, and network with big names, but none of this determines the quality of the individual's leadership. Leadership is a function of who you are and what you do, not what you wear, who you name drop, or how pretty your website is. There are only two ways to produce results in life: first, by production and second, by exploitation. Producers go out into the world and serve people to produce results for themselves and others. Exploiters cannot produce results so they quickly flock to producers in order to exploit part of the harvest from them. Producers and exploiters come in all shapes and sizes and in many different fields. Producers row the boat while exploiters are along for the ride.

Producers and exploiters have been in a constant battle since the beginning of time. Producers attempt to set up scoreboards to evaluate the true performance, while exploiters deceive themselves by flocking to jobs without scoreboards or even eliminating the scoreboard! If America is going to return to greatness, we must end the reign of self-deception and bring back true competition by keeping score, regardless of how politically incorrect this thinking may be today. China, India, Japan, and the rest of the world do not care a lick about our self-esteem and will destroy us in business if we do not compete. The beginning of all competition is to keep score and I emphatically encourage all businesses to start keeping score and evaluating results. Don't use words; don't deceive yourself by thoughts – show your results on the scoreboard.

Rush Straight In

You don't have a thousand years
To become who you're meant to be.
You have only a moment in time
An unknown fleeting quantity.
Drink deeply from the cup
Of life you've been handed
Taste all that's sweet
And endure what's bitter
Remembering the purpose
For which you've been born.
Squander not your days
Nor your gifts
Instead, arm them and
Send them into battle
To bring to life
Those quiet, hidden, but
True desires of your heart.
Never pull back from the flames
As cowards who conspire
But rush straight in
To your heart's desire.

"Winners hate losing more than changing while others hate changing more than losing."

"History can teach us so much, and yet we seem to learn so little."

"RASCALS ARE REASONABLE AMERICANS SEEKING CONSTITUTIONAL ANSWERS AND A LIMITED STATE."

"IT'S PROBABLY OBVIOUS, BUT TO LEAD, ONE MUST BE GOING SOMEWHERE."

"Every leader has the courage to make decisions. No decision is usually the worst decision."

"Do you see a problem in every opportunity or an opportunity in every problem?"

"THE RIPPLE EFFECT DEMONSTRATES THAT ONE PERSON CAN MAKE A DIFFERENCE."

"OVER TIME, HONESTY AND FAIRNESS GENERATE A MOMENTUM OF THEIR OWN."

"I stopped paying the price for success and started enjoying the price for success."

"POLITICALLY CORRECT" IS OFTEN "TECHNICALLY INCORRECT."

"Everyone starts life with a fire in their soul; sadly most are snuffed out in the storms of life."

"TRUE LEADERS STAND ON PRINCIPLE, NOT PLATFORMS AND PLATITUDES."

"IT'S ALL BEEN DONE, BUT IT HASN'T ALL BEEN LEARNED. THAT'S FOR SURE."

"WE GO IN THE DIRECTION OF OUR MOST DOMINANT THOUGHTS."

"Death is only a tragedy when life's purpose was left unfulfilled."

"THE GOV'T SNACKS ON THE COMPASSION OF ITS PEOPLE."

SAYING "AS SOON AS" IS A LOT LIKE SAYING "NEVER."

"Every uncomfortable experience in life gives you the choice of growing bitter or better."

Victim or Victor

There is an occupation that is experiencing significant growth. It has low entry requirements and can be had by literally anyone. Hordes are stampeding in that direction with noses acutely tuned to the smell of the gravy train. The position? That of "Victim."

Playing the part of Victim is becoming America's national sport. How could it be otherwise when it makes for such a perfect marriage between The State on one hand and Victims on the other? With a government fully vested in stoking the anger of its victim groups in order to secure more power for itself, institutionalization of victimhood is then well established. The proposition is equally attractive for individuals, because once claiming the status of a Victim, one is relieved of any personal responsibility. This is because victimhood bestows an entitlement: to blame others, to justify bad behavior, and to escape the consequences of one's actions.

There is another occupation with many positions available immediately. There is very little competition to hold these posts and again, anyone can apply. The position? That of "Victor."

Becoming victorious after a mighty struggle in pursuit of worthwhile purposes has a long and glorious history. Significance, contribution, service, love, and achievement are the rewards. Although many will give a silent head-nod in the direction of this occupation, few actually pursue it. With victimization so profitable, what's the point? Others languish in between, frozen between the two poles, wasting their time in complacent obscurity. But there are those wonderful Victors who choose to take personal responsibility and maximize their gifts by leaving the herd to pursue excellence. It is these who warm the rest of us to aspirations of our own. May we ever be thankful for Victors and their example.

WE ALL GET TO MAKE THE CHOICE DAILY.

May we choose wisely and become part of the solution group of Victors instead of the problem group of Victims.

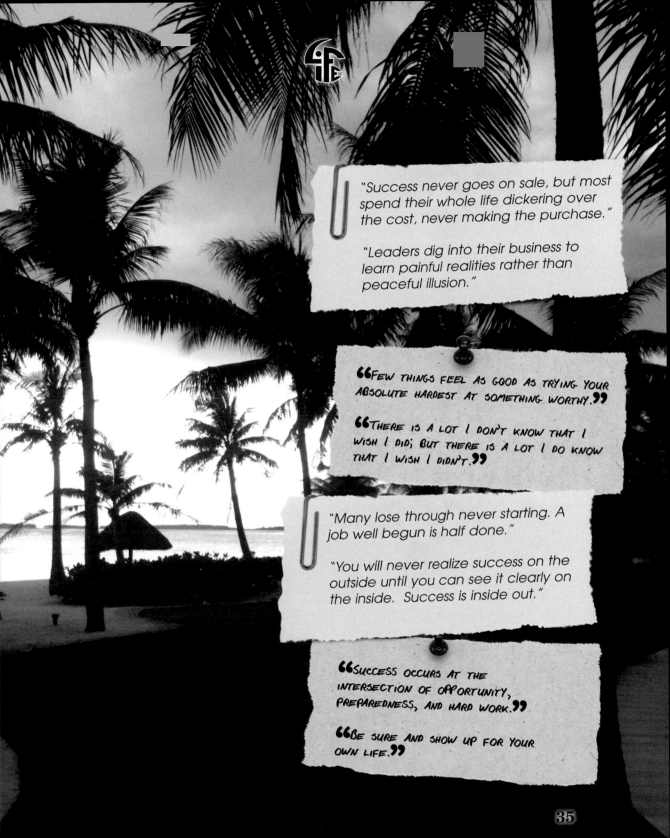

"Success never goes on sale, but most spend their whole life dickering over the cost, never making the purchase."

"Leaders dig into their business to learn painful realities rather than peaceful illusion."

Few things feel as good as trying your absolute hardest at something worthy.

There is a lot I don't know that I wish I did; but there is a lot I do know that I wish I didn't.

"Many lose through never starting. A job well begun is half done."

"You will never realize success on the outside until you can see it clearly on the inside. Success is inside out."

Success occurs at the intersection of opportunity, preparedness, and hard work.

Be sure and show up for your own life.

35

That Sparkling Mistress

Ah, art, that sparkling mistress
She winks at me through brick arches,
Marble columns and stone pediments,
Frescoes, sculptures, colors and forms,
Painstakingly extracted from genius,
Sinews straining against complacency
Languidly tempted to delay or do nothing.
What inertia must have been conquered
That you could have life.
What loving care must have been mustered
That you could long survive
To feel my gaze in an age that little notes
Nor barely understands what you represent.
The weight of the years past
A span of time beyond our easy comprehension
Is pierced by the remains of those heroes
Brave enough to unleash their talents
For at least a season of victory
Over their frail human nature
Driven to delay or squander
The impulse to give form to talent.
So much conceived and never begun
How much more initiated and yet still-born,
But oh, of what survived!
Of what made it through the dangerous passage
Between conception and completion
Surpassing all odds against fulfillment
Slipping past the weakness of the artisan
Into the sunny radiance
Of our latter-day appreciation.
A chilling reminder to us all
Of all that may still remain
Like Buonarroti's figure inside
Waiting for release from the block of marble.
And they ask me why I travel to Italy.

"But is the word used before you rationalize why the situation is not your fault nor responsibility."

"Everyone deals with the problems of life, but remember the goal is to solve them to get new ones."

Leaders must remember they become better equipped during their desert experiences.

Maybe we should be as wary of public officials as we are of public toilets.

"Leaders always choose the harder right rather than the easier wrong."

"A bitter heart is never thankful & a thankful heart is never bitter."

"Discipline is a given; the choice is whether it is applied internally or externally."

"The ability to focus is the key separation point between those who move ahead and those who fall behind."

If a fool and his money will soon part ways, how did they get together in the first place?

Hot air has served a purpose: it has built up steam in the freight train of political correctness and thought police.

Woe to the rascal who speaks out against 'conventional wisdom.'

Complex issues are untangled with simple principles.

The trick to success is convincing yourself you are worthy of it.

Great leaders are hard on themselves and easy on others.

"There are many shortcuts to failure, but there are no shortcuts to true success."

"Success is on the other side of your comfort zone."

37

Tell Me If Anything Was Ever Done

It at first seems odd that Leonardo da Vinci is so revered today. None of his sculptured works have survived, and only around a grand total of fifteen of his paintings are known. Although he wrote a lot about architecture, no buildings anywhere are credited to his name. Dispassionate scientists have long debated the originality of his many inventions found only in his sketchbooks – little evidence exists that he ever actually built or tested any of these ideas.

Yet Leonardo is heralded as a universal genius, the ideal of the Renaissance in which artists were not only proficient but expected to be masters in many fields. He is shrouded in mystery and myth, movies and books being written about his sensational secret codes, mischievous messages, and secret handwriting (which was actually just backwards).

As with most post-modern heroes, however, closer inspection reveals a somewhat smaller man. Although unarguably monumentally talented, Leonardo suffered from what art historian Ken Clark called his "constitutional dilatoriness." Pope Leo X said, "Alas! This man will never do anything!" Leonardo often accepted commissions for works he never finished, in many cases, works he never even began. Of the paintings we know of, such as the Mona Lisa, he worked on them off and on for years, most experts agreeing that the art itself shows the weaknesses of such a lackadaisical methodology. Perhaps authors D'Epiro and Pinkowish asked it best: "Why did the man who was arguably the greatest painter who ever lived dissipate his energies, often quite carelessly, among so many other fields?"

Let's address his current mass media popularity first: In our post-modern times, which seek any source of credibility against God and ultimate truth, Leonardo is a ready poster child for the Godless – possessing abundant talent and shrouded in sufficient mystery to speculate about alternate truths. In short, from a world-view that disdains accomplishment and merit (what one accomplishes and earns) and instead focuses upon position, power and prestige (who one is and who one knows), heroes are made out of those who seem to succeed despite the rules of effort, contribution, and earning it. Leonardo didn't have to accomplish much (in proportion to his gargantuan talent, that is) to be revered by those who don't really want to accomplish much themselves. Additionally, his atheism is seen as reassurance, as if to say, "If the great man didn't believe, then I can make myself great by being a disbeliever too."

But all that is really beside the point. There is absolutely no denying the fact that Leonardo da Vinci was an extremely gifted man, one of the towering giants of the Renaissance. The question that carries the most meaning for those of us on our own journeys of life accomplishment is "Why so little output?" I am reminded of the Stephen King quote concerning the author of *Gone With the Wind*: "Why didn't she ever write another book?"

SUCCESS IS THE PRODUCT OF MANY COMPONENTS, OF WHICH ONE OF THE MOST PROMINENT IS FOCUS.

We can do many things in our lives, but we can't do everything. We can have wide interests, and to a certain extent that is good and healthy, but we shouldn't dissipate our true well of talent on too many endeavors. If genius like that of a Leonardo is wasted by too broad a stroke, then what happens to those of us who are less well endowed? As Leonardo himself wrote, "As a kingdom divided against itself cannot stand, so every mind divided among different studies is confused and weakened."

I would posit that the less talented we are, the more focused we must be. Even the least talented can accomplish grandiose achievements if applying themelves ferociously, consistently, and with enough focus over time. In fact, it seems that often the greatest accomplishments go to those who actually aren't all that talented, but retain just this one last shred of talent: the ability to focus intensely and over the long term.

> Even the least talented can accomplish grandiose achievements if applying themelves ferociously, consistently, and with enough focus over time.

Sadly, we will never know what wonders of painted masterpieces Leonardo may have produced for the enjoyment of the world. He spent too much of his time elsewhere, on areas other than his gifting. While in many cases he was still better in these areas than most of the rest of us, the loss still stings. We are left wanting more, but time answers back a heartless "too late." This brings us to the saddest consideration of the squandered gifts of life: What could have been?

Do not squander what you've been given, no matter how much or little; rather, harness it, develop it, hone it, and focus it; bring it to bear on a daily basis and let the world see what you were given. It is a duty to return our gifts of talent totally spent and depleted in worthy use. Or, if not, one may join the great Leonardo da Vinci himself, who wrote toward the end of his life, "Di mi se mai fu fatta alcuna cosa." ("Tell me if anything was ever done.")

"Your past cannot stop you from a bright future, but an improper interpretation of your past can be fatal to your future."

"People will follow you when you build the character to follow through."

"THE TRICK TO LIFE IS ENDURING ITS INJUSTICES WITHOUT LOSING YOUR CHEERINESS."

"WHEN IT COMES TO DEALING WITH PEOPLE, ALWAYS TRY YOUR HEARTEST."

"Your dominant thoughts from your past have produced your today. Your dominant thoughts today will produce your future."

"You can tell the size of a person by the way he treats people who cannot help him."

"You must be willing to give up what you are, to become what you want to be."

"It's easier to teach a hungry person how to be sharp than it is to teach a sharp person how to be hungry."

Encouragement is the grease in the wheels of a team.

The common man pursues common distractions, and reaps the side effects. The uncommon man pursues uncommon aspirations, and reaps the rewards.

"You cannot expect others to believe in you until you believe in yourself."

"It's not about what you're capable of, it's about what you are willing to endure."

It's probably against the law to steal, because the government hates the competition.

The best leaders feel for their people as much as they burn for their goal.

"Champions do consistently what others do sporadically."

"If you accept excuses from others, it's usually because you have accepted your own excuse."

MOST PEOPLE DON'T REALLY KNOW WHAT THEY WANT UNTIL THEY SEE SOMEONE ELSE WITH IT.

IT'S HARD TO CONDEMN THE BEHAVIOR OF OTHERS WHEN YOU ARE REALISTIC ABOUT YOUR OWN SINFULNESS.

"Winning requires reaching inside of yourself for that extra gear to accelerate challenges."

"Those who row the boat don't have time to rock it while those who rock it don't have time to row it."

PEOPLE HIDE FROM THEIR DESTINY INSIDE ALL MANNER OF DISTRACTIONS.

IF YOU PUT OFF THE IMPORTANT STUFF LONG ENOUGH IT WILL ULTIMATELY LEAVE YOU WITH NO MORE CHANCES.

WE DON'T KNOW WHAT WE DON'T KNOW.

A Leader's Biggest Enemy

Great leaders are the first to admit they don't know all the answers. You may have heard it said that we don't know what we don't know. Also, we have forgotten a lot of what we used to know. Worse, however, is the fact that we know a lot that just isn't so.

Beware those who think they have a lock on truth, who push their agendas on others with arrogant disdain, and who are blind to their own failings. The greatest leaders don't make these mistakes. They know they don't know all the answers, and that is part of what gives them so much hunger to learn more. Where most give platitudes, great leaders give their own example.

Seasoning and experience are keys here. This is because youth tends to be wrapped in untested confidence. Age, however, can bring cynicism and surrender. Somehow, the best leaders navigate between these two and proceed confidently but humbly. It is a fine line, indeed.

So lead bravely. Go boldly into new territory. Just make sure you've got control over the most rebellious follower of all: yourself.

> Where most give platitudes, great leaders give their own example.

Everyone deals with problems in life, but remember: the goal is to solve them and get new ones.

I know something about you. That's right. It's not a secret, so you might as well admit it: you have problems. The good news, if we can call it that, is you're not alone, as everyone goes through times of struggle. In fact, if you are breathing you have problems. Maybe it's time to move past the problem step and start reaching for solutions, learning so you can move on to the next assignment. My (Orrin's) wife, Laurie, has a beautiful statement she likes to share, "The lesson continues until the lesson is learned." Life is not meant to be lived camping out on Lesson One, fearing life is too difficult, hiding to avoid problems; it's supposed to be a grand adventure involving dreaming, struggling, and having victories along the way. The more quickly one solves the current lesson the sooner one advances to new heights, achieving more results with each progressively higher lesson number. If you're going to have problems anyway, my suggestion is to make life interesting by solving a few problems, gaining new ones, solving some more, and gradually and eventually producing results of which you can be proud. The secret to success lies in your daily habits. Champions solve problems daily, producing adventure and results to last a lifetime. What are you waiting for? Identify the issue to be addressed and start solving it today.

> *Champions solve problems daily, producing adventure and results to last a lifetime.*

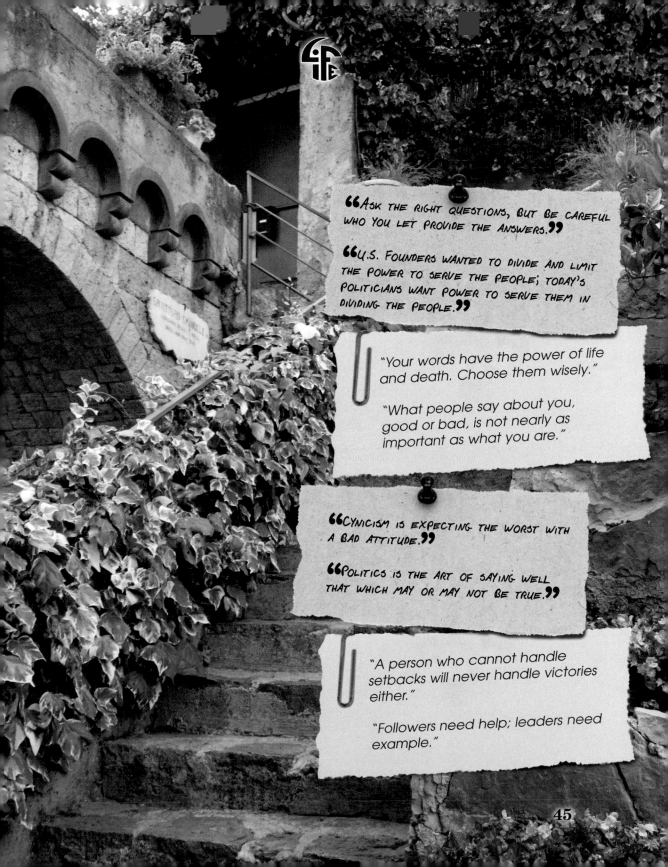

"Ask the right questions, but be careful who you let provide the answers."

"U.S. Founders wanted to divide and limit the power to serve the people; today's politicians want power to serve them in dividing the people."

"Your words have the power of life and death. Choose them wisely."

"What people say about you, good or bad, is not nearly as important as what you are."

"Cynicism is expecting the worst with a bad attitude."

"Politics is the art of saying well that which may or may not be true."

"A person who cannot handle setbacks will never handle victories either."

"Followers need help; leaders need example."

"Success comes from will, not skill."

"Freedom's ends are not (or should not be) selfish ones."

46

How Are the Others Doing?

It stopped me dead in my tracks when I (Chris) read it. As a result, I put the book down and couldn't come back to it for days. When I finally did, I was still stunned by the revelation of my inadequacy.

What was it that shot like a lightning bolt of illumination into my blinded mind? The statement that "to determine how well you are doing as a leader, take a look at how well the people you lead are doing."

Ouch.

To that point, I had been thinking I was a leader when actually I was operating only at the lower level of "performer." It was all about me, my goals, my performance, my motivation, my accomplishments. I thought that if I drove myself hard enough, learned enough, and tried enough, I would be a good leader. Unfortunately, that's not how it works.

As we wrote in *Launching a Leadership Revolution*, leading involves much more than that. Leadership is the art of influencing other people to high performance. It is the power of a performer enabling and enhancing the performance of others. And therein lies the key: OTHERS.

Want to be a leader?

Want to increase your influence?

Want to take your performance to the next level?

Become OTHERS focused. Decide right here and now that your life will not be about you, but about others. Figure out how to add more value to more people with everything you do. As Zig Ziglar famously said, "Help enough other people get what they want and you'll have everything you want." This statement, I believe, is both literal and figurative. I DO believe that by helping others succeed it boomerangs back around and helps the helper. However, the deeper and more figurative meaning is that by helping others get what they want you receive so much more. You receive their thanks and gratitude, adulation and respect, friendship and loyalty, comfort and presence. Just by being the "raiser" of others you have been raised yourself.

> *Help enough other people get what they want and you'll have everything you want.*
> – Zig Ziglar

So make your work and life about others.

How they do is the gage of how you are doing.

"People will not change their minds, but they will make new decisions based upon new information."

"Success, for most people, requires unlearning as much as learning."

66 THE BEST TIME TO PLANT A TREE IS 20 YEARS AGO. THE 2ND BEST TIME IS NOW. TRUE FOR FINANCES TOO. 99

66 WHEN IT COMES TO FOOD, HASTE MAKES WAIST. 99

"Belief is the magic key that unlocks your dreams."

"Most people live with pleasant illusions, but leaders must deal with hard realities."

66 IT IS VERY DIFFICULT TO GET A LAWYER TO SAY THE SAME THING TWICE, OR GET TWO LAWYERS TO SAY THE SAME THING ONCE. 99

66 MONEY SHOULD BE OUR SLAVE, NOT OUR MASTER. 99

"You cannot expect your team to rise above your example."

"If the only thing that you are good at is convincing others that you are good, then being in biz with you is bad experience."

66 DISORDER IS A DANGEROUS DISEASE THAT EITHER CLUTTERS OUR ACTIONS (BUSYNESS) OR SOLIDIFIES OUR HESITATIONS (IDLENESS). 99

66 ONE OF THE MOST IMPORTANT WORDS IN THE ENGLISH LANGUAGE TO DEFINE PROPERLY IS 'SUCCESS.' 99

A Sentinel In

"Winners see the dream and develop plans while the rest see the obstacles and develop justifications."

"The only place where compensation comes before service is in the dictionary or anywhere the government meddles."

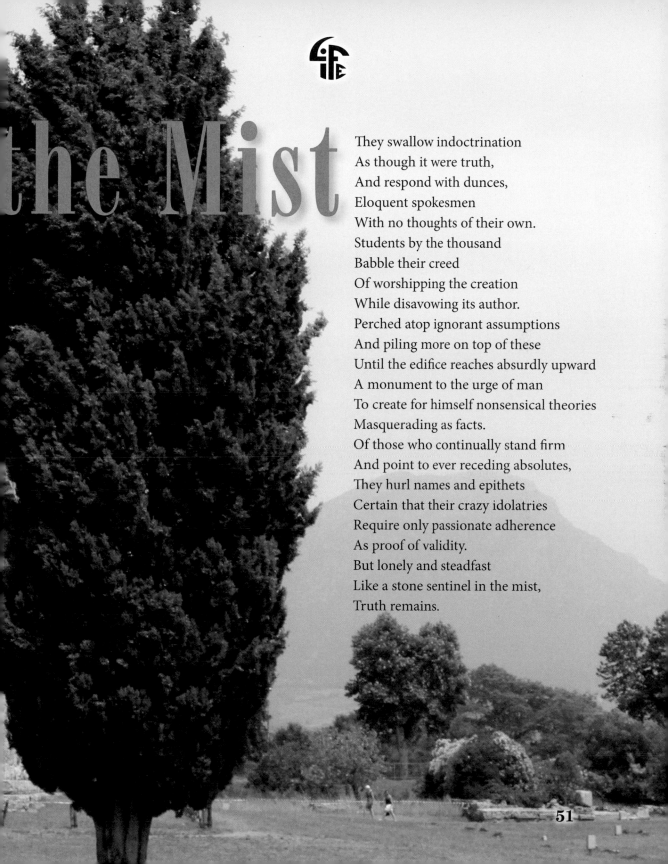

the Mist

They swallow indoctrination
As though it were truth,
And respond with dunces,
Eloquent spokesmen
With no thoughts of their own.
Students by the thousand
Babble their creed
Of worshipping the creation
While disavowing its author.
Perched atop ignorant assumptions
And piling more on top of these
Until the edifice reaches absurdly upward
A monument to the urge of man
To create for himself nonsensical theories
Masquerading as facts.
Of those who continually stand firm
And point to ever receding absolutes,
They hurl names and epithets
Certain that their crazy idolatries
Require only passionate adherence
As proof of validity.
But lonely and steadfast
Like a stone sentinel in the mist,
Truth remains.

"Average leaders raise the bar on themselves; good leaders raise the bar for others; great leaders inspire others to raise their own bar."

66A RASCAL IS AN ORIGINAL CHARACTER; ONE WHO CAN'T BE CLASSIFIED, MINIMIZED, SILENCED OR ENSLAVED.99

66WINNERS PLAY HURT.99

"A low self-image is usually not based upon facts; it's mismanaged memory."

66RASCALS ARE REBELS WITH A CAUSE.99

"Doubts in your mind are a much greater roadblock to success than obstacles on the journey."

66SMILE AND PEOPLE WILL THINK YOU KNOW WHAT YOU'RE DOING. FROWN AND PEOPLE WILL THINK YOU KNOW WHAT THEY'RE DOING.99

66IF WE KEEP THOSE TWO PARTIES IN WASHINGTON, THEY WILL KEEP PARTYING IN WASHINGTON.99

66NO FOCUS, NO MASTERY.99

"Life is meant to be lived in 'the zone', not the stands."

66THERE IS NO SAFETY IN A SIGNIFICANT LIFE, AND THERE IS NO SIGNIFICANCE IN A SAFE LIFE.99

"Encouraging free people to notice and appreciate their freedom is like telling fish about water."

"Dreams must be strong for accomplishments to be mighty."

"Managers maintain an efficient status quo while leaders attack the status quo to create something new."

"Until you accept responsibility for your life, someone else runs your life."

"It takes merely seconds to destroy the character that years were required to build."

"Distraction has the power to derail the accomplishment of nearly anything."

"Without courage, it doesn't matter how good the leader's intentions are."

"The passion/hunger of the student brings out the experience/wisdom of the mentor."

"Many vigorous beginnings lapse into careless ends."

"Unless you are training to be a victim, take the bad things that happen to you as God's way of developing your character."

"One person with commitment accomplishes more than a thousand with an opinion."

"Anlaysis paralysis occurs when you overthink and underwork."

"A nation of sheep begets a government of wolves."

"Problems are the price of success."

"Education is a lifetime assignment & terminates when you do."

"Too many non-achievers confuse humility with humiliation."

RAISING THE BAR

W hat is it about leadership? It seems as if the more we talk about it the harder it is to understand. It is a topic that refuses to be quantified and escapes our airtight definitions, no matter how many hours we spend on the subject. But all of us know when leadership is present, and sadly, when it's not. When a leader moves, the team moves, accomplishing record-breaking outputs, while creating cultures that produce results for the long term.

> **When a leader moves, the team moves...**

Attempting to define leadership reminds me of the story of the blind men who were feeling different parts of the elephant. When attempting to describe what they were feeling they described a truthful summary from their own perspective, but certainly not an accurate record, because each was missing huge parts of the overall picture. If we take any of the blind men's description as an all-inclusive answer, we will be led astray and will miss huge parts of the picture.

An average leader raises the bar on himself by pushing past his former limits. Internally driven to improve, he settles for nothing less than his personal best, achieving more by believing more, breaking his previous records. Since example is so important in leadership, modeling the proper behaviors for the rest of the team becomes one of a leader's key assignments. He accepts no excuses from himself or others, constantly seeking to drive leadership improvement. Example alone will move a team forward but will not create championship organizations.

A good example which confirms this principle is Michael Jordan's early professional career. By driving himself to fanatical levels to improve, holding himself accountable to the highest standards, he achieved personal success at the peak levels, winning multiple scoring championships, but regretfully, no team championships. The joke around the league nicknamed the Bulls: "Michael Jordan and the Jordanaires." Being a top performer in one's field is not enough; building a winning team requires more, such as the ability to empathize with others, to listen to their fears, and to coax the greatness out of them. Jordan eventually became a champion, not because his personal skills improved, although they did, but because he learned to play as part of a team through the influence of Phil Jackson. Jackson taught Jordan key lessons that all top performers must learn, mainly, to be patient with the weaknesses of others, to empathize with their fears without sympathizing, while consistently inspiring them with their dreams. Jordan learned to lead on the court, including the team more by sharing the ball, and in essence playing the lead instrument, but not the only instrument, in the

Bull's five-man basketball band. The Chicago Bulls went on to win six NBA championships, a phenomenal feat in any sport, especially the grueling game of NBA basketball.

Leaders must help raise the bar on others by expecting more, believing more, and allowing others to do more. Remember, individuals grow, but teams explode. Winning teams form when everyone on the team is increasing his or her skills through the influence of leadership. Wherever you see a team growing, whenever you see an organization breaking through, it is for certain that a leader was hard at work raising the bar on his or herself and on others.

The highest level of leadership, an extremely rare level, achieved by only a few individuals in any particular field, is when the leader inspires other leaders to, in turn, develop more leaders. It's tough enough to perform, tougher still to perform while leading others to step up their game, but dynasties are created when leaders surround themselves with other leaders, raising the bar of excellence throughout the organization. Leadership at the highest level demands a lifetime of serving others, surrendering recognition, serving unconditionally for years, and believing in people when everyone else has given up on them. True leadership then, is less of what you *do* and more of who you *are*. People follow you because they know you are trustworthy; because you have proven yourself over the years to be who you say you are.

Leaders willingly sacrifice in the short term for long term results.

AVERAGE LEADERS RAISE THE BAR ON THEMSELVES; GOOD LEADERS RAISE THE BAR FOR OTHERS; GREAT LEADERS INSPIRE OTHERS TO RAISE THEIR OWN BAR.

I love the old saying, "If you are growing tomatoes, plant for a season; if you are growing oak trees, plant for a lifetime." Top leaders deny the urge to control others, realizing that leaders do not need to be controlled. Instead, top leaders inspire others with compelling character and vision, so other leaders align to achieve greatness together. Dynasties are created when people buy into the team's vision, exchange personal ego for team ego, demand excellence from themselves, and compel others to raise their own bar. This is the top, the peak of leadership, which creates a vision from the mountaintop, a culture of excellence, and the birth of a dynasty.

"WE ARE HAPPIEST MAKING OTHERS HAPPY."

"FOR THOSE WITH POOR FINANCIAL DISCIPLINE, A LACK OF MONEY IS NOT THE PROBLEM, THEREFORE MORE MONEY IS NOT THE SOLUTION."

"Every right that we enjoy has a corresponding duty to not interfere with the enjoyment of the same right by others."

"A leader is always first in line during times of criticism and last in line during times of recognition."

"INTERDEPENDENCE IS INDEPENDENCE TO THE POWER OF TEAMWORK.**"**

"LONG-TERM VISION IS THE POINT ON THE HORIZON AT WHICH TO AIM. DELAYED GRATIFICATION IS THE SELF-DENIAL REQUIRED TO GET THERE.**"**

"The only thing you can take with you when you die is what you are. Character counts more than possessions."

"IF YOU DON'T TAKE FULL RESPONSIBLITY FOR WHERE YOU ARE, YOU'LL NEVER BELIEVE YOU HAVE FULL POWER TO GET YOURSELF WHERE YOU WANT TO GO.**"**

"Most people overestimate others' talents and underestimate their own."

"COMFORT ZONES ARE MIS-NAMED; THEY SHOULD ACTUALLY BE CALLED 'FAMILIAR ZONES'. THEY MIGHT NOT BE COMFORTABLE AT ALL.**"**

"A person that does not value your time will not value your advice."

"THE WORLD MIGHT ACTUALLY CHANGE IF MORE PEOPLE FOCUSED ON CHANGING THEMSELVES INSTEAD OF THE WORLD.**"**

"LEADERS MUST NAVIGATE BETWEEN RECKLESS CHANGE AND LISTLESS COMPLACENCY.**"**

"LIFE HAS NO REWIND OR RESET.**"**

"A leader must inspire or his team will expire."

"Those who serve deserve."

57

IMPROVEMENT DEFICIENCY SYNDROME

There are excellent books on how to improve our lives in all areas. There are wonderful seminars conducted by some of the sharpest minds about how to identify our blind spots and grow personally. Mentors and coaches and helpers who encourage people on pathways toward self-improvement are plentiful. But even though these incredible enablers of positive change abound, there is an all-too common disease that thwarts all the greatest efforts toward lasting self-improvement, and it is called: Improvement Deficiency Syndrome (IDS).

Improvement Deficiency Syndrome occurs in both men and women, old and young, across seemingly every demographic and socio-economic sector. IDS appears early in some, has a late-onset in others. The symptoms of IDS include the following:

1. Persistent resistance to a positive attitude
2. The ability to read hundreds of self-improvement books and still not improve
3. Inborn selfishness that exhibits itself with repeated flareups
4. Sudden anger and jealousy and the "taking of offense" based on some obscure behavior of other people
5. Pervasive self pity and the justification necessary to feed it
6. The making of excuses to cover one's lack of advancement
7. The continued placement of self at the center of the universe
8. The ability to see any self-serving action as justifiable and righteous

Yes. These symptoms are serious.

If you or anyone you know appears to be exhibiting these effects, see your mentor immediately. If you detect that being in a positive environment, reading good books, and associating with uplifting people is having no effect on your attitude, heart, or service toward others – seek help fast. You may be a chronic sufferer of IDS.

Beware the sufferers of IDS. Such people are among the most self-deceived of our species.

Don't take this lightly. Already, hundreds of thousands of people around the world have been identified as having symptoms of IDS. It has destroyed friendships, ruined marriages, and derailed careers.

The trickiest part about identifying the presence of IDS is that the afflicted person, having read so many good books and having associated with positive people, knows how he or she should be behaving. This leads to effective masking, as the person with IDS "fakes" the correct behaviors to cover up for his or her lack of a growing heart. Bad attitudes are hidden under false smiles; anger and jealousy are shrouded in an artificially positive attitude; selfishness and self-pity are positioned behind a platitude of positive sayings and cryptic one-liners.

Beware of the sufferers of IDS. Such people are among the most self-deceived of our species. They think by doing the right things they are becoming the right person. They mistake deeds for development, actions for intent, and works for heart. They think saying and doing the right things is what it's all about, instead of thinking and feeling and becoming the right person. In short, they think by *acting* better they actually have *become* better.

Should you encounter sufferers of IDS, pray for them immediately. Administer love and support, but be firm in your insistence that they seek help. Although the serious debilitating effects of IDS can explain their behavior, it can never be justified. Get them to see their mentor immediately, and apply heavy doses of tough love and an insistence upon a change that takes place deep inside, at the heart level, spiritually. Nothing less has ever been found to work.

> Should you encounter sufferers of IDS, pray for them immediately.

"If you aren't loyal to the few you won't be blessed with the many."

"The problem with incompetence is its inability to recognize itself."

"Life is too short to learn the same lessons over and over again."

"If you're fighting for something that matters, the obstacles don't."

"Leaders speak truth into people who believe lies about themselves."

"Everyone carries a bucket of water and a bucket of gas in life. A leader has learned to throw the right one at the right time."

"Do what you can, the best you can, while you can, even though some days the can will get kicked."

"The principal thing is to follow your principles."

"Bad habits: easy to develop and hard to live with. Good habits: hard to develop and easy to live with."

"Sight is seeing with the eyes; vision is seeing with the mind."

"The right decision is sometimes not the safest."

"Either own up to your mistakes or they will own you."

"When the urgent crowds out the important, people urgently accomplish nothing of value."

"'Do you have the talent?' is rarely the question. 'Do you have the guts to finish?' is the real question."

"People have high belief in their own thinking; low belief in their own abilities."

"Success comes from the accumulation of correct efforts over time."

"Leverage is the ability to apply positive pressure on yourself to follow through on your decisions even when it hurts."

"It's not what you eat that will kill you as much as what is eating you."

61

CUL-DE-SAC

How many times has it happened?
Arranging and scurrying around,
Seeking the arrival
That seems more illusive than justice?
Full speed ahead,
Don't they say fortune favors the bold?
But halting abruptly
As we must if we are to keep our sanity
Finding ourselves in another Cul-de-Sac.
The sprocket kicks off the chain,
As our feet slip from the pedals.
Thank God for the asphalt
Because at least we can put our foot down to restart.
I wonder about the running tally
Of turnabouts in my life
Shifting into reverse
And rolling over the refuse of costly mistakes,
Investments in nothing more than passing fancy
Now handed off at one-third the price.
But they had so captured me at the time
Flashes of shine catching my eye
Deviation from the magnetic pull
Weak though it is
Toward my scripted route.

Veer here and veer over there,
Zigzagging my way through days
Always confidently pursuing
The next memory to be found only in pictures,
Captured digitally and flickered on a screen.
There's no program for rewind
A subroutine never compiled
So all we can capture from each Cul-de-Sac
Is the lesson expensively bought,
But soon forgotten by eyes too weak to focus
On anything but vapor?
Destiny knows better, though,
Than our vanity and flimsy whims
The ticking of the clock as we sleep
Reminding us of how much we have spent
And how little we have to show for it,
But then again, so much,
Somehow crafted from mistakes,
A life complete and filled.
We run right by what we really need,
Into the next Cul-de-Sac,
Chasing what we want,
And getting what we were supposed to
All along.

❝Being in business should not mean being in 'busyness.'❞

❝Looking outward to find someone to serve is the roadway out of adversity.❞

"You don't feel like a winner and then do; you do like a winner and then feel."

"Leadership Principle: As hunger increases, excuses decrease."

❝The business of government should not be business.❞

❝Intellectuals are those people who make complicated explanations against common sense.❞

"Don't be your own worst critic; there are plenty of other people willing to fill that position."

Maybe you aren't the best at what you do. Don't let that get you down, only one person can be the best at any endeavor. The real question is, "Are you getting better?" The key is to keep growing, striving to become better, personally and professionally, at whatever God has called you to do. Many people become their own worst critics, beating themselves up mentally, anguishing over lost opportunities; but you cannot change the past. Stop looking in the rear-view mirror while attempting to move forward. Leaders learn from the past, act in the present, and accomplish in the future. Most people suffer from analysis paralysis, dwelling on the past, but not acting in the present. Remember, it's called the Book of Acts in the Bible because the apostles acted on the message, not just thought about it. You cannot seize your future until you are willing to let go of your past. Examine your past, looking at the good, the bad, and the ugly, pondering what better choices could have been made, learning the lessons, but then moving on. When you stop being your own worst critic, leaving the past in the past, achieving successes like never before, someone else will volunteer to fill the critic's position. Like the old saying goes, "The higher you climb the ladder of success, the more your butt is exposed."

"Discipline is joyfully enduring the things you don't want to do so you can consistently enjoy the things you do want to do."

"A person who refuses to stay down will eventually wind up on top."

"IT'S NOT WHAT YOU SAY, IT'S WHAT THEY HEAR."

"THE RELATIONSHIPS IN YOUR LIFE SHOULD BE SOME OF YOUR MOST PRIZED 'POSSESSIONS.'"

"Focus is the ability to concentrate on the majors even when the minors invade your space and time."

"You will not do the work if you do not believe you will achieve the victory."

"THE ONLY BAD EXPERIENCE IS THE UNEVALUATED EXPERIENCE."

"ONCE SOMEONE LOSES BELIEF IN HIS ABILITY TO ACHIEVE SOMETHING, HE LOSES THE DRIVE TO ATTEMPT IT."

"All people respond to challenges creatively – some think up solutions, others think up excuses."

"The best way to read a person's mind is through his or her actions."

"If you want to move on in life, replace bad habits that hold you back with better ones that propel you forward – Give up to go up!"

"In leadership, the cause always comes before the applause."

Do not let the friction of living wear away your cheeriness.

Many people appear to be tip-toeing through life trying to get to death safely.

"Most people wear themselves out thinking about doing the work instead of just doing it."

"Champions are in a constant never ending quest for excellence in all areas of life."

Our government acts as if it has memory loss: staring at a fire it caused, wondering how it got started!

We cannot fix what we cannot clearly define.

Lighten Up and Toughen Up

There are two attitudes toward life that I (Chris) think are paramount for leaders, especially in our modern, pampered times. They are:

1. Lighten up
2. Toughen up.

There is nothing more off-putting than a person who takes him or herself too seriously. One of my favorite phrases is, "Take everything seriously except yourself." People can easily get a little too "heavy" with the bearing of their burdens. Remember: everyone has problems. Nobody's health is perfect. Nobody's relationships are all perfect. Nobody has it made. You shouldn't be surprised when you don't, either. So lighten up a little bit, and work on your attitude. Become more fun to be around. Look at the bright side of things. Find the silver lining in every storm cloud. Trust me: you will be remembered for how well or poorly you do this. People flock to those who are positive, full of enthusiasm, and large on life. They run from the dour, sour, complaining, serious, "realistic" types. So make your choice to lighten up.

Also, there are few sights more pathetic than a person having a pity party. For the most part, the people walking the earth today have more blessings, better health care, better nutrition, better shelter, longer life expectancy, more opportunities, easier travel, more time-saving devices, etc., than anybody has ever had before, including kings of the highest power. (This is not to downplay the condition of those who are truly suffering from the absence of even the basic necessities of life. But most people reading this are not of that category, but rather, are blessed beyond description.) We should realize how relatively easy our lives are, and rejoice in the blessings God has provided. This ought to toughen us through our challenges, give us the proper perspective, and make us stronger. Nobody likes a wimp.

> *We should realize how relatively easy our lives are, and rejoice in the blessings God has provided.*

There you have it: two of my favorite admonishments. As you make your way through your day today, ask yourself, "How can I both lighten up and toughen up?"

"Learn from the past, live in the present, lead into the future!"

"Confronting areas to change is uncomfortable for a season, but not confronting is uncomfortable for a lifetime."

Strong sailors are not made on calm seas.

There are a lot of really nice people in this world. And a few others.

"Leaders must learn to prioritize the important from the urgent or they will urgently go nowhere."

"Rules without relationships equals rebellion. – Put relationships first!"

Humor can be found in almost every aspect of life. I believe the primary reason for this is because life is full of humans.

Most people act as if life is linear, when it's actually a little crooked.

68

"The worst decision is indecision."

"Self Discipline is the ability to do what you don't want to do. Self Control is the ability to not do what you want to do."

DON'T BE LIKE EVERYONE ELSE. EVEN IF YOU'RE THE ONLY ONE.

SHORT TERM ACTIONS HAVE LONG TERM CONSEQUENCES.

"Practice doesn't make perfect. Only perfect practice makes perfect."

"Entering the race is half the battle because you cannot finish what you are unwilling to start."

I THINK THE GENE POOL NEEDS SOME CHLORINE.

WHEN YOU ARE TRYING TO CHANGE THE WORLD, BEWARE OF THOSE WHO ALREADY RULE IT.

Hiding From Destiny

Do you believe in destiny? We do. We believe that each one of us was given special talents and a calling all our own. We all know it deep inside. It's there when we are quiet enough to listen, when we shut off the media, the noise, and the busyness. Perhaps it scares us. Perhaps we don't think we're worthy. Maybe we don't want to be held responsible. But it's there.

> We believe that each one of us was given special talents and a calling all our own.

So why do so many run from it? Why are ears plugged and eyes tightly closed against any possibility of the greatness of our inner potential? Why do we suppress the divine spark with decadence and shallowness?

We decided to tabulate a list of the things that people hide behind in order to avoid the doing of what they were put here to do. It's a farcical tale acted out by idiots, who are beautiful but flagellate themselves to keep anyone from discovering it. They fasten down tightly the bushel over their light.

Here's our list. Feel free to get offended, or add to it (or both). Your choice. Look closely, though, and you'll see thousands of people hiding behind each of these, maybe even someone you know.

1. Victimhood
2. Sickness
3. The burning need for money to satiate pathetic spending habits (materialism addiction)
4. Self-dramatization and the over-amplification of problems
5. Relational combat
6. Media fixation/entertainment binging
7. Addictions
8. Behavior designed to gain attention
9. Failure and the need for pity
10. Self-deception
11. Self-sabatoge
12. Laziness
13. Debauchery
14. Psychological escapisms
15. Sports fanaticism
16. Career
17. Status
18. The pleasing of others/approval fixation
19. Fear/timidity/doubt
20. Procrastination
21. Distractions of all stripes
22. Poor focus
23. Lack of introspection or meaningful thought

Make the decision to wake up now.

Hide behind nothing. Face your destiny and charge after it with all you've got. You'll never feel better, have more fun, or make more of a difference any other way. After all, you're supposed to be all you can be! Nothing less will do.

"If you are going to play the game anyway, play the game to win."

"Character is doing what is right regardless of what you want."

America: the land of people with get—up—and—go descended from those who got—up—and—came!

Life has no rewind, but it is being recorded.

"Just as pain is weakness leaving the body, failure is ignorance leaving our game plan."

"Stop trying to think your way into new actions and start acting your way into new thinking."

Competition is the gymnasium of discomfort from which stronger participants emerge.

Don't squander your difficulties; wring every possible lesson out of them!

"Leaders can either organize a plan to win with their team or agonize over the failure of their team."

"A leader is said to have charisma by habitually taking a greater interest in others than in themselves."

The best experience is someone else's, properly examined and applied.

Leaders must understand that as supply creates demand, courage creates progress.

"Everyone succeeds up to the level of his or her limiting belief."

"Winning happens by learning from every loss and making the necessary course corrections."

Many leaders begin a great journey, but few finish.

Know-it-alls are really just people with bad attitudes about the competency of others.

"Leadership is more about inspiring and less about requiring."

"Character is more easily kept than recovered. It takes years to develop and can be lost in minutes."

66 THERE IS, HAS BEEN, AND ALWAYS WILL BE DIGNITY IN HARD WORK TOWARD A NOBLE END. 99

66 THE UNIFORM OF LEADERSHIP IS THICK SKIN. 99

"Leadership is not delegated person to person, but is acquired the moment responsibility is accepted."

"The best way to impress others is to genuinely be impressed by them."

66 THE SADDEST EXCUSE IS THE ONE A PERSON SELLS HIMSELF. 99

66 IF WE WERE BLESSED WITH LESS, WOULD WE ACCOMPLISH MORE? 99

MOVE OR LOSE

THERE ARE TWO REACTIONS people exhibit when confronted with challenges. The first is the most common. It involves the wearing of a long face, the art of moping, and the self-protective mechanism of retreating into one's shell. Picture a *rolly polly* bug. At the first sign of trouble he curls up in a ball, hoping nobody can see him and hoping beyond hope that some snot-nosed toddler doesn't pick him up, roll him around, and ultimately squish him. I'm not sure why this is the case, but when people come under financial pressure specifically, their reaction is usually the exact opposite of what it should be. Their reaction to the problem amplifies the problem instead of erasing it. They become paralyzed, their activity slows down, they over-think every angle of their situation, and, in short, they haul off and do a lot of nothing.

The second reaction is the correct one. It involves the taking of massive action against the problem. It is the old maxim, "It's time to do something, even if it's wrong." This reaction may or may not be perfect, but because it involves action it usually leads to adjustments over time and therefore becomes more and more productive. As it has been said, a car is easier to steer once it's moving.

"It's time to do something, even if it's wrong."

Action is the key. Character is exhibited by the action of the individual in the face of paralyzing pressures. When the average person would curl up like a bug, the champion comes out swinging. Never underestimate the power of massive action to initiate a whole train of events that can pull you out of your problem. Its cumulative impact is often hard to believe. Progress stacks upon progress, challenges recede, breaks seem to happen in an increasingly positive direction, and the sky begins to clear.

But none of that will happen if you sit on the couch, mope, blame, or stay paralyzed by your problems. Get up and get moving. The world is passing by and takes little notice of those who play the victim.

Quit losing and get moving.

ACTION IS THE KEY

"Most people overestimate what can be accomplished in one year and underestimate what can be accomplished in ten years."

"Poor leaders are like broken umbrellas. They elude discovery when the sun is shining, but reveal their ineptness when it rains."

TRULY HIGH PERFORMANCE REQUIRES A CAUSE BIGGER THAN ONESELF.

A CYNIC IS A DISAPPOINTED IDEALIST.

AMERICA'S #1 SPORT? SPENDING MONEY.

"True greatness requires endurance as much as talent."

"What you say to others is a good read on what you are saying to yourself."

WE GROW AS WE SERVE.

NEW IDEAS ARE DANGEROUS TO THOSE INVESTED IN THE STATUS QUO.

LIFE IS BEST LIVED AS AN ADVENTURE.

"Inside of you is the character to rise and win or to surrender. Which you choose during the struggles determines your destiny."

"Mentorship – affirms the person while suggesting a different thought perspective."

IT'S YOUR BUSINESS TO KNOW WHAT BUSINESS YOU'RE IN

It should go without saying that you should know what you're doing in order to do it. But a surprising number of people and even companies don't seem to know what their main purpose is. There are two groups, however, that can always be counted on to understand this perfectly well: 1) customers and 2) competitors. One will leave you and one will devour you if you don't figure it out.

So what business are you in?

Have you clearly defined it?

Are you sure that's really it?

The answers to these questions are important because they dictate the strategies, decisions, and actions that lead to results, or lack thereof. **These are not trite exercises — they are paramount.**

Let's take Steve Jobs of Apple Computer fame, for example. He is a subject worthy of study, to be sure, having succeeded tremendously at an extremely young age, then floundered famously, only to rise from the ashes and soar to ever higher heights. I will, at some point in the future, do a more in depth write-up on this interesting man, but for now it will suffice to use him as what I hope will be a clear example of the main point of this article. (Aren't you glad there's a point?)

The very name of "Apple Computer Corporation" gives a hint to where I'm going with this. You see, I contend that part of what was amiss with Steve Jobs in his first run-up to success was that he didn't understand the nature of his own genius. He thought he was in the business of making and selling computers. Following this purpose sent him down many cul-de-sacs and eventually led to his ouster from the very company he helped launch.

He fared even worse at his "next" adventure, NeXT Computers, in which he focused again on building and selling computers, this time to a slightly different market. But along the way he did a few things correctly, which morphed into his eventual success and return to the top. Most importantly, he either discovered or just simply got aligned with his overall true ability: making technology incredibly, reliably, and stylishly useful to the average person.

You see, most of us aren't really interested in how a computer works, or the intricacies of programming, or the cleverness of a sub-routine. I have been alive for the entire computer revolution, my first exposure to it being at my friend Ramana's house in fourth grade where he showed me his P.E.T. computer.

"What's it for?" I asked.

"For computing stuff," he replied.

"Like what?"

"Well, you can write lines of programming code and it will compile it," he answered.

"Can we play with your Star Wars action figures some more?" I asked.

Computer technology has always been interesting to the Ramana's of this world, but not to the rest of us mere mortals. (Ramana would go on to be a valedictorian.) For the most part, my experience with computers has been a forced, frustrated exercise in learning detailed gobblygook I didn't want to learn in the first place. I just wanted the end result of what the stupid thing was supposed to produce.

Enter Steve Jobs. With his sense of cool and his near maniacal insistence that things "just work," he stands like a knight in shining armor for all of us who desperately need technology but find it no more interesting than putting bamboo shoots under our own fingernails. The fact that he could bring us something that works, and even make us feel cool doing it, was his real genius. I contend, in fact, that it's the real business he's in. Once he discovered this fact he has been unstoppable. This realization broke him out of the box of "making and selling computers" and led him into the world of digitized music (iPODs and iTunes), computer-animated full-length feature movies (Pixar), and computing devices that serve our lives reliably (MacBooks and iPhones). Good job, Steve. Although you think Zen is cool and don't eat meat, I still can somehow relate to you.

So tear a page out of Steve Jobs' playbook, or at least sing to one of his tunes on your iPod Shuffle, and get it clear in your head what your real business is. If you think it's as simple as providing a functional-based answer like, "making and selling widgets that people want to buy," you deserve what's coming to you. But if you can truly discover your genius angle, that likely you and only you can provide, then you'd better prepare for a moonshot. There will always be a market when you get it right.

SO WHAT BUSINESS ARE YOU IN? HAVE YOU CLEARLY DEFINED IT? ARE YOU SURE THAT'S REALLY IT?

Mob or Team?

A mob of people is one of the most dangerous and heartless entities on earth. Conversely, a team of highly functioning and productive people is one of the most heart-warming and inspirational. The difference is leadership.

Few things have ever been accomplished by the lone striver. People must combine into productive groups and each contribute their best to a team effort for real accomplishments to occur. In this way, the whole far exceeds the sum of the parts. Participating on such a team can be one of the most liberating, exhilarating experiences in life. Productive teams are not only fun to be a part of, they are also responsible for just about everything in our civilization, from technological advancements to architectural wonders to sports dynasties.

The most highly functioning teams are aligned in common purpose, for a noble cause, and work respectfully and trustingly together. They are more concerned about the glory of the team than they are about personal accolades. They take care of each other and push each other to higher contribution, in an "iron sharpening iron" way. Peer pressure becomes a positive, and heights are reached collectively that would be beyond the ability of any individual.

Great people are required for great teams. But there is something more. Many times the most "talented" groups do not perform as predicted. Leadership is required to form and lead teams to higher and higher achievement, and it is this leadership that makes all the difference.

LEADING TEAMS TO EXCELLENCE REQUIRES INTENTIONALITY AND HARD WORK, CONSISTENTLY APPLIED, OVER TIME.

It requires the leader to clearly and continually develop group themes to which everyone ascribes. It requires vision and consistency, fostering of harmony and trust, confronting issues that threaten the cohesion of the team, and a nourishment of the belief that what the team sets out to do it in fact can do.

As the old saying goes, "Put two idiots in a room with an expert, and after a period of time, three idiots will emerge." So it is with teams. Even the most talented groups of people can become corrupted and callous if left untended, without true leadership and guidance administered on a regular basis. Leadership is the force that prevents the mob tendencies of any group of people and instead channels those energies into productive alignment. And this leadership can come from any and all levels. Just because one isn't the titular head of an organization of people doesn't mean he or she cannot lead. Any position is in touch with other parts of the team and therefore exerts a certain amount of influence on the rest. A strong leadership example of the right things always has its effect. So lead mightily from whatever position in which you find yourself, and contribute to the smooth functioning of your team. Without it you can expect mob-like behavior. With it, you can expect the absolute best. The choice is yours.

"A leader truly listening to his or her team speaks more than any talk given to them."

"A big secret to life is when you learn that learning is just as entertaining as entertainment, but with long term benefits."

One of the saddest things to see is a life lived selfishly.

Massive action against calamity is not only an effective response, but a restorer of sanity.

"There are two classes of things you should not worry about: 1. What you can help. 2. What you can't help."

"Fulfill your potential & some may abuse you, but don't fulfill your potential & you abuse yourself."

Adversity is not something you should merely try to get through, but rather grow through.

A long term vision not only provides direction, but motivation for the journey.

"In today's world of feckless & fickle friends, give friendship based upon fidelity & faithfulness."

"Before people will see value in you, they must first feel valued by you."

66 SUCCESS IS LIKE RUNNING UP A DOWN ESCALATOR. THE MORE THE GOVERNMENT INTERFERES, THE FASTER THE ESCALATOR RUNS AGAINST US. 99

"When you starve someone's stomach, they become ornery; when you starve someone's ego, they become angry."

"A huge part of winning in life is how quickly one goes from problem identified to problem solved."

66 'REGULATION' IS THE GOVERNMENT'S ANSWER TO EVERY PROBLEM — LIKE A DRUG ADDICT TAKING ANOTHER HIT. 99

66 A GOOD BOOK IS HARD TO READ, ON ACCOUNT OF HOW OFTEN IT MAKES YOU STOP AND THINK. 99

Leaders Travel Light

I learned it the hard way, really, by dragging bulky bags through crowded bus terminals, onto packed trains, and up stairs at a five-hundred year-old hotel. I will never forget slugging two huge suitcases through Narita station in Tokyo, stopping at a trash can and throwing a way a bunch of stuff to lighten my load.

My (Chris's) wife and children have bought into this dogma unbelievably well, packing for a month in Italy and needing only one suitcase amongst the five of them! Running shoes and a miscount of pull-ups (We had enough with us to make a raft and float back home across the Atlantic.) took us up to a total of two.

Traveling light is not only a necessity for anyone wanting to do some serious traipsing around the globe, but it serves as a valid metaphor for life, as well. Let's face it, there are those who just cut a large swath through their life, traveling heavy and weighing things down. While there are others who seem to flit from episode to episode without exacting a heavy toll on those around them.

Leaders often go into unfamiliar territory, influencing others to follow them there.

Leadership is a lot like taking a trip. Leaders often go into unfamiliar territory, influencing others to follow them there. Leaders must provision themselves and their people for the journey. Leaders must be ready for and respond properly to the obstacles and challenges that inevitably come. The best leaders are the most agile, the most able to adjust and course-correct, the most rock-solid on commitment to a vision but the most flexible on the route. Leaders build trust and develop networks, alliances, and deep relationships. And of course, the best leaders have character and integrity.

All of these can be seen as features of traveling light through life. Though leaders may carry heavy and often unfair burdens, they do so with grace and fidelity to a worthy cause, which means that they have to carry little else. Here are some areas to consider when seeking to increase your leadership ability by traveling light:

1. Relationships – heavy is the burden of broken and un-repaired relationships. Light is the load of tight friendships, deep bonds, and heart-felt trust.

2. Commitments – heavy is the burden of too many commitments or casual ones made without thought or conviction. Light is the load of commitments to God-given principles and worthy goals. While some of the heaviest loads of all are those made up of shards and splinters from commitments we've broken in life.

3. Focus – heavy is the load for the leader who is unable to focus and prioritize accordingly. Light is the load of a leader who understands that almost anything can be accomplished if enough focus of energy, desire, concentration, talent, effort, perseverance, time, and toil is applied. You can accomplish almost anything you truly commit to, but you can't accomplish everything. You must choose, and then attack with everything you've got.

4. Honor – heavy is the load of the person who cannot be trusted, breaks promises, fails to keep confidences, and cannot be relied upon. Such people will find life getting tougher and tougher as the accumulation of those who know them for what they are grows. Worse than the accumulated opinion of those let down is the searing pain of a burned conscience within. Perhaps the heaviest load to carry is one of guilt and regret.

> The best of leaders are like the best of travelers; they travel light.

5. Principles – heavy is the life that doesn't stand for anything except selfishness, self-aggrandizement, and personal glory. Light is the life given over to the glory of God, service to others, and the fight for good.

The best of leaders are like the best of travelers; they travel light. Like the good traveler who takes nothing but pictures and leaves nothing but tracks, the best leaders take nothing but responsibility and leave nothing but love and example.

BECOME THE BEST LEADER YOU CAN BE: TRAVEL LIGHT.

"Never surrender convictions for conveniences."

"America will remain free only as long as people desire freedom over security."

Anything worth doing well is worth doing poorly until you can master it.

Our privileges aren't for our pleasure but for our purpose.

"Being a critic is much easier than being a leader as it requires no sacrifice or results."

"Today's age worries too much about image and not enough about integrity."

Commitment is the wedge that drives open the door of momentum.

"The courage to do is in shorter supply than the knowledge of how to do."

The safe life is the riskiest one of all, because it risks the wasting of itself.

"True unity turns average talent into a great team while disunity turns great talent into a poor team."

"People who defend themselves are not sorry and people who are sorry do not defend themselves."

It's hard to get down when you're looking up.

"Managers operate through control of people while leaders operate through inspiration of people."

A critic is like the girl that can't dance, so she says the band can't play.

"You will either let your dreams overcome your fears or your fears overcome your dreams."

84

List to the Lee

No rewind on life
Our grasp has no grip
There's not a thing we can do
To slow down this trip.

Open your eyes wide
See all that you see
Gales blow to the rocky shore
We list to the lee.

We kick against goads
Blame struggle for pain
Totally blind to the point
That hurt reveals gain.

For how could we know
That all that we want
Elusive and misleading
In this lifetime jaunt?

For if we caught it
Our tail in our teeth
Would we stop and just wonder
If time slipped the sheath?

Our empty pursuits
Our grubby hand-holds
Will only fail to secure
All that's dear we hold.

A deeper yearning
Tugs soft at our sleeves
We hide under a bushel
Ignore what it means.

But it's there for good
For our greatest gain
And sometimes we find it most
When in the most pain.

It's our true calling
Our life's one purpose
That carries us home again
Safe harbor's purchase.

The hound of heaven
Viciously runs down
Many strivers and dreamers
When they've hit the ground.

Keep your eyes upward
Use your strength to chase
Eternal not temporal
Or your life you'll waste.

Only You Can Stop You

We've studied for years the many people who have achieved tremendous things in life, and one thing I find common to them all is the audacity to follow their own inner voice. If you think about it, much of our unhappiness comes from wrong turns and calamitous dead-ends that result from us not really knowing what we want.

Just how did you become trapped in that job you can't stand? What made you get so in debt? How did you become over-burdened in commitments you didn't really sign up for? When you are unclear about what you really want out of life, there will be no shortage of people who will quickly rush in to fill the void. "Oh yeah? Don't know what you want, huh? No problem, WE know what we want from you. Just step right over here . . . ."

Decisions are only difficult if you don't know what your purpose is.
– Lou Holtz

Lou Holtz once said, "Decisions are only difficult if you don't know what your purpose is." Stated another way, I might say it like this: "Unhappiness and a lack of fulfillment may result from not knowing what your purpose is." Not to mention the squandering of talents, wasting of time, and loss of opportunity.

So listen to that inner voice. Follow your passions and hide not your light under a bushel. You were built for a purpose. When it comes down to it, you are the only one who can stop you.

LiFE

"Success requires a time of sacrifice for a period; failure requires a lifetime of sacrifice – period."

"If necessity is the mother of invention then frustration is the father of progress."

"Dig your heels in and fight the current of mediocrity. You can do better."

"As Christians, our relevance is based on our reverence, not in conforming to this world."

"It's what you learn after everyone else believes you have 'arrived' that keeps you on the journey."

"I would rather do nothing than be busy doing nothing."

"If we are too comfortable in this world, we won't be in the next."

"Darwin had it wrong. We aren't descended from apes; there's more evidence for sheep."

Take Time

"Take time to smell the roses," it has been said. The spirit of this quote is correct, I feel. However, I am not sure about that "take time" part. If you think about it, there is no such thing as "taking time." Time just is. It clicks along at a terrifyingly steady pace as we go about our business. Time won't stop, pause, halt, or even slow down. In fact, the older I get, the more I'm convinced it speeds up. Time itself is almost impossible to define. Perhaps it's a measure of existence from the perspective of how much of it has already gone by. Nowadays a year feels like three months. In a decade or so? Well, mere minutes, I suspect.

I received word yesterday that a business associate passed away suddenly. From all outward appearances he was otherwise in perfect health. Gone. Just like that. I am saddened for the loss felt by his family and friends, and I am hopeful that he knew the Lord and Savior Jesus Christ as his own. Also, his death causes me to think the deep questions that often hide out at the far extremes of my consciousness. Things like this tragic news seem to chase those thoughts out onto center stage, overpowering their bashfulness and forcing them to be clearly seen. I am reminded of our mortality, of the brief stop-over that this life is, and the purpose we are to serve while here. Stop. Think. Pray. Then be about what it is you were created to be about. Only you can do what only you can do. So stop wasting time waiting, arranging, planning, scheming, or preparing. Get busy being and doing. And while you're at it, hug someone you love and let them know how you feel. Who knows, it just might be your last chance.

Freedom tends to foster prosperity while regulation tends to impoverish.

Realistic self-assessment is the starting point of productive personal growth.

"Changing the external environment is not nearly as important as changing the internal, because wherever you go, there you are."

"Blaming someone else for your failures only ensures that you won't learn from them."

The citizens are responsible for making the government worthy of its soldiers' sacrifices.

Hurry is the enemy of inspiration.

Inspired contribution requires a moral cause.

"One moment of God's favor is worth a lifetime of my labor."

"A man helps himself, a wise man helps others."

When all is said and done, there is usually more said than done!

The only way to be happy is to give happy!

"Appreciation of people returns a greater harvest than appreciation of money."

"You can do anything by keeping the main thing everything, but you can do nothing until you focus on something."

OBJECTS IN CALENDAR ARE CLOSER THAN THEY APPEAR.

EXPERIENCE IS SOMETHING YOU DON'T GET UNTIL JUST AFTER YOU NEED IT.

"I would rather have a thousand 'no's' on my way to victory than one 'I told you so' on my way to defeat."

"Honor is doing what is right even when you have the power to do wrong."

YOU CAN BANK ON ANY FRIENDSHIP WHERE INTEREST IS PAID.

IMPATIENCE IS INEVITABLE FOR PEOPLE WHO LIVE ONLY IN THE PRESENT.

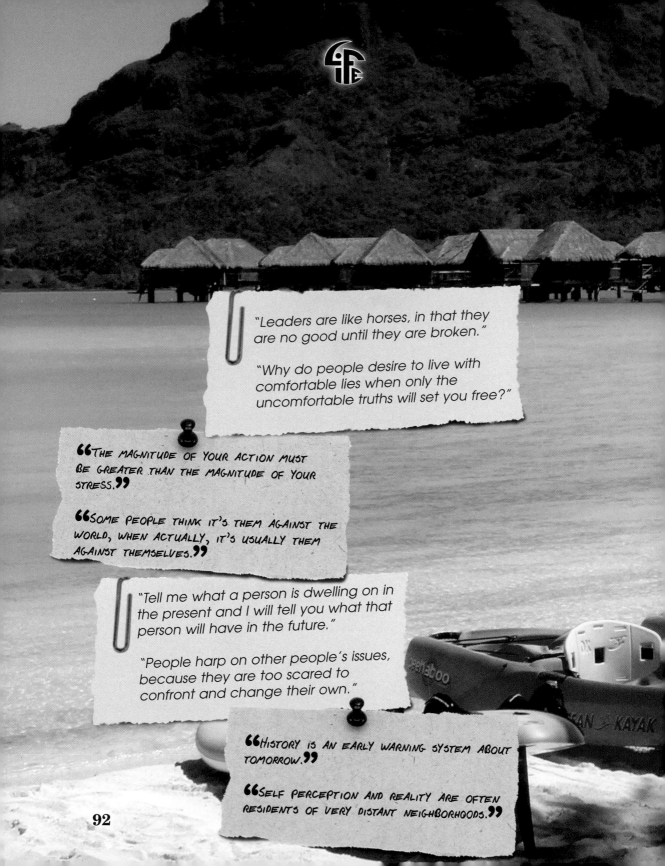

"Leaders are like horses, in that they are no good until they are broken."

"Why do people desire to live with comfortable lies when only the uncomfortable truths will set you free?"

The magnitude of your action must be greater than the magnitude of your stress.

Some people think it's them against the world, when actually, it's usually them against themselves.

"Tell me what a person is dwelling on in the present and I will tell you what that person will have in the future."

"People harp on other people's issues, because they are too scared to confront and change their own."

History is an early warning system about tomorrow.

Self perception and reality are often residents of very distant neighborhoods.

92

A Life That Risks the Wasting of Itself

Success doesn't happen by accident, and if it does, it's not really success and it won't last. True success happens on purpose. It results from the accumulation of enough of the correct things done properly, over time. In other words, it is intentional.

So what?

Well, we must realize that this isn't as obvious as it sounds. If it were, more people would be making intentional steps toward the realization of something great, instead of bilging on distractions and wasting their days.

What's the holdup?

Belief. People will only do what they believe they can do. Once they start to get doubts they also start to stop. This is why our world is crammed full of starters but crying out for finishers.

So work on your mental picture of what you want to accomplish, who you want to become, and what you feel God has designed you to do. It's not okay to tiptoe through life trying to get to death safely. The safe life is the riskiest life there is, because it is the life that risks the wasting of itself.

> **People will only do what they believe they can do.**

93

"GROWN-UPS" SHOULD MAKE SURE THAT THEY HAVE

Children are wonderful, bright-eyed, positive, full of ideas, and as curious as can be imagined. Truly, they are a blessing from God. However, any time I want to understand a little bit of human nature, all I have to do is observe them from a different angle.

In addition to all the good things we practically idolize about children in our culture, there are many of the uglier sides of humanity on display, as well. These include selfishness,

possessiveness, emotional immaturity, short-term focus, and a lack of taking responsibility for their actions. It is characteristics like these, when displayed in "adults" who should know better, that are most bothersome.

Take, for instance, the concept of stewardship. This is the concept that the "things" we have are gifts and should be cared for accordingly. Included in this list are our physical bodies and health, our finances, our relationships, and the world in which we live. Children are not very good stewards of anything; this is apparently because stewardship is something that must be learned. Children live through their days with nary a thought about their physical diet, muscular development, money, friendship maintenance and cultivation, and the environment. Let's take that last category of "environment" as an example: children leave messes everywhere they go, leave lights on, waste food, leave water running, and a whole host of additional behaviors that would make Al Gore wince. I could go on.

In short, while we can learn a lot from our children about the bright side of humanity, we can probably learn just as much about the darker side. In the area of stewardship we adults should work at becoming better caretakers of all we've been given. Neglect not your health, your relationships, or your planet. In all things, excess is usually wasteful and destructive, negligence is irresponsible, and apathy is pathetic.

In conclusion: as "grown-ups," we should make sure that we have.

"Focus everyday on closing the gap between the person you are and the person you want to be."

"Proper mentorship provides you with a new perspective on your challenges & the encouragement to tackle them anew."

A PALM TREE GROWS BY REACHING UPWARD WITH NEW GROWTH FROM INSIDE, WHILE OLD STUFF ON THE OUTSIDE DIES AND FALLS AWAY.

EXCELLENCE ALWAYS SUCCEEDS; IT'S JUST A MATTER OF WHEN, HOW, AND HOW BIG.

"The best predictor of your future is what you do with your free time."

"As a leader, does your team feel better about themselves and their abilities to get the job done after associating with you?"

WHEN IT'S TIME TO WORK IT'S TIME TO WORK; WHEN IT'S TIME TO PLAY IT'S TIME TO PLAY. DO YOU DRAW SUCH LINES?

PROFESSIONALS FOCUS ON THEIR CRAFT TO THE EXCLUSION OF ALL DISTRACTIONS. ONLY THEN ARE THEY FREED UP FOR ANYTHING ELSE.

Busyness, Snake Oil Salesmen, and Execution

In all of the talk one finds today regarding leadership, there is one aspect in particular that seems to be assumed (and often times erroneously). That one thing is execution.

Productivity is a foundation stone for the credibility a leader must garner in order to influence others. There is no shortage of people who can act busy, be busy, get busy, or seem busy. There is also no shortage of people who have themselves convinced that because they work hard they are therefore effective.

Productivity is a foundation stone for the credibility a leader must garner in order to influence others.

Busyness, however, is merely a snake oil salesman at the back of a rickety cart promising lotions and potions for all sorts of tricks. Sometimes, the potions work. After all, isn't real medicine itself a type of potion? But for the snake-oil salesman, most potions are mere hoaxes. That is what activity and busyness are. Sure, success requires hard work and busyness, effort and at times long, arduous hours. However, much of what passes for hard work is no more than a false elixir made to fool (often to the highest degree) the person who himself is doing the work.

Don't fall for the con of your own activity level. Many, many people are busy, but it is the rare person who executes efficiently and effectively, considering priorities, living by the 80-20 rule, and posting results time and time again.

Are you good at getting things done?

Do you execute compellingly?

Can you be counted on to finish what you start?

When given responsibility for a task, can you be trusted implicitly with its efficient and complete performance?

If not, you may consider your lack thereof as a limiter on your influence and credibility with others.

Just saying.

"WINNING IS FINE AS LONG AS IT DOESN'T GO TO YOUR HEAD. LOSING IS FINE AS LONG AS IT DOESN'T GO TO YOUR HEART."

"PERSEVERANCE: THE QUALITY THAT IS THE HARDEST TO MUSTER WHEN YOU NEED IT THE MOST."

"You cease to be excellent the moment you accept mediocrity in your life."

"Success is the exponential effect of little things done consistently over time."

"IF YOU DO NOT EXERT DISCIPLINE OVER YOUR FINANCES, YOUR FINANCES WILL EXERT DISCIPLINE OVER YOU."

"Leaders know that no one changes until they are willing to, but that anyone can change when they are willing to."

"YOU CAN'T HELP WHERE YOU COME FROM, BUT YOU CAN HAVE A SAY IN WHERE YOU'RE GOING."

"IF YOU GIVE MORE THAN IS EXPECTED YOU JUST MIGHT GET MORE THAN YOU DESERVE."

"Mastery involves linking the pain of the process to the birth of a better you."

"MANY TIMES YOUR RESPONSE TO A PROBLEM IS MORE IMPORTANT THAN THE PROBLEM ITSELF."

"PEOPLE SHOULD LIKE THE WAY THEY SEE THEMSELVES WHEN THEY LOOK THROUGH YOUR EYES."

"People follow passion and principles, not possessions."

"IF YOU DON'T WANT TO DO SOMETHING, NOBODY CAN STOP YOU!"

"Winners think and act while others talk and watch."

DON'T THINK THEY DON'T

I (Chris) was a newlywed at the time. That should explain a lot. Also, I had grown up doing dangerous things in a world that hadn't yet caught the "safety addiction."

For instance, when I was a kid it was considered quite normal to be carted around town in the back of a pickup truck, ride in cars without seat belts, hold your baby on your lap in the front seat (Our car had baby-bite marks in the vinyl door panel to prove it!), play with lawn darts, ride three wheeler ATVs, mow the lawn without hearing protection, sit in a pinch-your-fingers metal high chair, burn leaded gasoline, ride in the back window of a car, pour your used motor oil out at the end of your driveway, siphon gas with a garden hose, burn your trash in a barrel in your yard, use lead paint, attend schools featuring asbestos pipes, paint a car in your garage without OSHA approval, skateboard without pads, get spanked with Dad's belt, walk to school (both ways, up hill, in the snow), sit two inches from the television, drink water from the tap, and ride a bike without a helmet.

As I write this, some of these are cracking me up. Others seem quite trivial. The least of these, at least at the time of my "newlywededness," was the bike helmet one. I just didn't get it. I had raced motocross, off-roaded Jeeps and trucks, Jet-Skiid the waves of the Great Lakes, and any number of moderately risky things. Of course, with few exceptions, I'd participated in these activities while adorning the proper safety equipment. I'd even done a fair bit of mountain biking and had, of course, worn a helmet. But riding a bike around a paved neighborhood? Why in the world would I need a helmet for that?

Married less than a year, we had just moved into our first official home. The sunny summer afternoon beckoned us outside and we pulled our bikes from amongst the stacks of boxes yet to be unpacked. I was about to open the garage door when my wife said, "Aren't you going to put on your helmet?"

"What?" I said, incredulous. Surely she was joking.

"Come on. Just wear it. It's about safety."

"Safety? Are you kidding me? We're going for a little leisurely ride on flat, paved streets! I've never worn a helmet when biking, ever! Only on tough trails and stuff."

"Honey," she reasoned, "just wear it. It won't hurt to be safe, and besides, it'll set a good example for the neighborhood kids."

"Neighborhood kids? You've got to be kidding me! They aren't our kids! And besides, they won't even notice a couple of adults casually riding by on their bikes. No way!"

Showing the grace her husband would (hopefully) someday learn, Terri let it drop. We raised the garage door and rode out onto our short little driveway. We couldn't have made it ten feet when the three year-old neighbor girl loudly proclaimed, "Hey! Daddy! How come HE doesn't have to wear HIS helmet!?"

> When it comes to influencing people, example isn't the main thing, it's the only thing.

I couldn't believe my ears. How my wife kept from saying "I told you so" is beyond me.

No matter who you are, where you live, or what you do, someone is watching. Importantly, it might be your own children, loved ones, friends, and/or relatives. It may even be strangers. Quite possibly, it will be the three-year-old girl next door.

Example is a funny thing. Whether you want to have one or not, you do. It is not optional. It is simply there, every minute of every day of your entire life. Never underestimate the power of your own example. As Albert Schweitzer is often credited with saying, "When it comes to influencing people, example isn't the main thing, it's the only thing." While this might be an oversimplification, the sentiment is worth considering.

Give careful thought to whom you may be influencing (and how) on a daily basis. Who is watching you? What do they see? If they had to give an evaluation of your behavior, what would they say? Are you a model worth copying? Are you coming across the way you think you are? Or, in the clearest of terms, are you who you say you are? Are you even who you think you are? Whether you want to admit it or not, people watch, absorb, and copy (or reject) you. Don't think they don't.

"Success is not as easy as winners make it look, but it's not as hard as losers make it sound either."

"If you want to achieve more, you will need to expect more, do more, and become more."

"Leaders need courage to make decisions that affect a small number of people negatively and a large number positively."

"Praising people in private is good, but when done in front of peers it is life-changing for all."

It has been said that the life of a great achiever can be summed up in one sentence. Think about what yours might be.

Better said, 'Life in the Zone' wears no watch.

"The best way to make a positive impact is to develop your gifts so you can share them with the world."

"America needs leaders to innovate, motivate and elevate the teams in every organization."

Time loses its predominant tyranny over us when we are in full pursuit of our calling (i.e. we don't notice it).

Things are sometimes exactly what they seem.

WORKING AT THE ROOTS

Bob mopped and mopped but couldn't seem to make any progress. The water just kept flowing, flooding his laundry room and seeping out into the rest of his home. Nearly exhausted, mops soaked, water still flowing, only then did Bob consider the source of the water. A quick inspection revealed a split pipe just below the sink. With decisiveness and speed, Bob turned an upstream valve and stopped the flow of water. Within seconds the stream of water that had previously been constantly soaking the floor dribbled to a stop. With one last mop Bob was able to eradicate the last spilled water and remove the final traces of moisture from his laundry room. Shaking his head in wonder, Bob couldn't believe how the pressure of the emergency had distracted him from attacking the problem at the source. He was only glad his wife had not seen his hour-long dance with insanity!

> We must develop the belief that problems can be solved.

The above is a rendition many have used to illustrate the fallacy of becoming distracted by the symptoms of our problems instead of focusing on their root causes. This succinct parable is so simple and so obvious that we think it could never happen to us. Of course we should turn off the source of the water. Who wouldn't? But yet the world is full of people chasing symptoms and ignoring causes. Entire industries exist to treat symptoms, convincing people that they are at least "doing something" about their problems. But we must develop the belief that problems can be solved. It is not enough to be "doing something," we must learn to do the *correct* things.

Leadership success is largely dependent upon the leader's ability to think through situations and arrive at root causes.

In short, the best leaders identify problems, then solve them. Let me say that again: the best leaders
1) Identify problems, and then
2) Solve them.

This makes perfect sense. It is obvious. It is so simple that a grade school student could understand it. But don't rush past the seemingly elementary. Stop and consider that very few people ever develop the ability to identify root causes. Even fewer learn to solve them. But solving problems largely stems from properly identifying their root causes. Therefore, put enough energy into step 1), and you're well on your way to accomplishing step 2). It is for this reason that a leader must have the discipline to do the hard work of thinking through the tough issues in order to define them properly. Thinking of this type is hard work, and, as Henry Ford once quipped, "Thinking is the hardest work there is. That's why so few people engage in it." But a leader does not have the option of avoiding this difficult work. In fact, this IS the work of a leader.

What are the top five problems assailing you and/or your organization at the moment?

Have you done the hard work of (continually) thinking through these issues?

For each, have you identified the root causes behind the aggravating symptoms?

Are you expending resources and energy fighting symptoms that only appear to be causes?

Problems can be solved if and when they are properly identified and confronted head-on.

> *Thinking is the hardest work there is. That's why so few people engage in it.*
> – Henry Ford

Learn to work at the roots and the leaves will take care of themselves.

Friendship: The Obscure Obvious

Scan any book store and you'll find millions of books on how to make more money, thousands about how to be more spiritual, hundreds about how to be a better wife and mother, and maybe five or six on how to be a better husband and father. Rarest of all, however, and relegated to the skinny shelf-space reserved for titles such as "Honesty Among Politicians" and "Government Thrift," you may occasionally find one or two books on friendship.

Friendship.

It's a word familiar to us all. Just hearing it evokes an immediate understanding of what is meant by the term. No definitions are required. We understand, got it, get it, and own it. Or do we?

In my life, I have been blessed with many friends. But more and more as I age I have come to discover that a true friend is one of life's rarest finds. What passes for friendship among most is no more than familiarity through some shared experience, membership, or proximity. I have experienced (as I am sure has every reader) people who claimed to be or acted like friends who behaved in the most un-friend-like manners. I won't elaborate. Rather, I'd like to focus upon what should be obvious aspects of friendship in an attempt to shine light into this strangely obscure genre.

You make Friends easily

First of all, friendship is an unofficial, mutually beneficial relationship involving at least two parties. Friendships generally start spontaneously or casually and blossom into more as bonds are built and commonalities are discovered. But everything can't be in common: some of the best friendships grow out of complementary trait alignments.

Second, friendship requires giving and taking on both sides. As long as the exchange maintains some sort of balance, the relationship can continue. Anything too one sided is no longer friendship. There must be flexibility and tolerance, forgiveness and grace extended in both directions.

Third, friendship should be fun. After all, we can always get around people whose company we don't enjoy. (Insert any number of in-law or family reunion jokes here.)

Fourth, friendship should be relatively easy. It's not that a good friendship won't require some maintenance and uncomfortable moments at times (which can actually serve to tighten bonds of trust and respect), but for the most part, friendships should be a comfortable load in an otherwise strenuous world. We have enough people in our lives with whom we are forced to maintain some sort of relationship; we don't need our friendships to be sources of strain.

Fifth, and perhaps most importantly, friendships can only exist on a foundation of trust. Many casual relationships carry most of the features above, but when it comes right down to it, the parties can't actually and fully trust each other. Not so for true friendships. In true friendships, trust is a must.

Let's review, then, these obvious traits: **mutually beneficial, balanced, common, complementary, flexible, tolerant, forgiving, grace-filled, fun, easy, comfortable, and trusting.**

Now, if you'd like to get a clearer picture of the friendships in your life, simply write down the five people who you consider to be your "best friends." Think carefully about this. Make sure they satisfy all of the above attributes.

Were you able to come up with five who totally satisfied the list? Many people can't. When we really stop to consider the features of friendship, a concept we often take for granted, we begin to realize just how rare a true friend actually is.

Look at the list of attributes again. Now ask yourself how well you satisfy them for someone else. Who do you think would put you on their list of five?

Want to have better friends? Be a better friend. How? By examining the above list of features and remembering to be those things for another person.

Anonymous Friendship Quotes:

A friend is someone who knows all about you and loves you anyway.

The best mirror in the world is a true friend.

True friends are difficult to find, hard to leave, and impossible to forget.

A true friend is one who thinks you are a good egg even when you're half cracked.

A friend will help you move, but a true friend will help you move a body.

"Most people have problems with integrity because they cannot keep promises to themselves, let alone others."

"Telling a person to seek a nice secure job would be like telling a lion in the jungle to seek a nice secure zoo."

Do you know what you are trying to accomplish today, or are you just plowing through?

Freedom ruins a man for slavery ever after.

"I have witnessed two minutes of encouraging words change a person's life. Sadly, I have witnessed discouraging words do the same."

"90% of excellence is achieved with 10%. 10% of excellence requires 90% of effort but produces 90% of the results."

Leaders can only expect what they inspect.

The pursuit of success through decadence offers few roadblocks; try succeeding at something worthy, however, and watch out!

"Most gifts are temporary and over time whither away; cars rust, clothes tear, diamonds can be lost, but ideas change lives forever."

"Just because those around you surrendered their dreams does not mean that you should."

It is truly amazing the length to which people can go to justify their own misbehavior or lack of performance.

I am also convinced that one should never attempt to write a history book without including at least one map!

MOTIVE-ASSIGNERS VS. BENEFT-OF-THE-DOUBTERS

Have you ever considered just what we mean when we say, "He seems like a pretty nice guy?" Does it mean he has good manners, is kind, friendly, amicable, and easy to get along with? Most likely. Does it also mean he is slow to anger and quick to laugh? Also likely.

Allow me to add another aspect to the mix of those whom we consider to be "nice." There is a subtle behavioral difference among people, I find, and it involves a choice in how to interpret the actions of other people. Here is what I mean.

You are in traffic, in a rush to get somewhere, and suddenly a slow driver pulls out in front of you with no apparent care in the world. Operating entirely on a difference clock speed than you, the person forces you to sit through red lights you'd otherwise have made, and no matter how you try, you just simply can't get around him or her. How do you react? Do you fly into a rage and begin reciting the relative demerits of their ancestors? Do you take it in stride and just go along with the flow, realizing there's not much you can do to change their pace? Or do you react somewhere in between? "They're doing that on purpose!" you might conclude. "They pulled right out in front of me just to spite me!" you think. Perhaps your reaction depends upon the circumstances of your day, your mood, and the position of the moon relative to your mother-in-law. That is all understandable. But allow me to finally get to my point, which is this: when confronted with frustrating behavior (to you, at least) on the part of another person, do you generally

1) Give them the benefit of the doubt, or
2) Assign a motive to their behavior?

Your answer to this question, I believe, has a lot to do with whether or not people consider you to be "nice," or otherwise.

"That jerk did that on purpose!" you might say or think. "He did this, which means that, and he knew darn well that . . . ." or "He should have done this if he wanted me to . . ." or "I know what he really meant by that," and the list of examples goes on.

Some of the "nicest" people I know, who have therefore become great friends of mine, are people that seem to usually choose response number 1). They are slow to assign illicit motive to the behavior of others; they demonstrate a level of patience with other people's actions; and they are slow to pass judgment. Others, with whom I have sometimes temporarily been in association, seem to predominately choose response 2), in which they automatically assign motives and reasons to the behavior of others. Rarely, if ever, are these motives positive. It is as if they think they have an incredibly acute clairvoyance, which allows them to both clearly understand the reasons for another person's behavior (when that person may not even understand his behavior much himself!) and to draw conclusions from that behavior which reflect wider consequences. "He's doing that because blah blah blah, and that can only mean he thinks blah blah blah."

Our society is actually quite genteel. It is difficult to get away with behavior that is too rude or openly obnoxious. Therefore, many people have learned to shield these "motive assigning" thoughts a little bit. They appear kind and gentle on the outside, but inside they are world-class motive assigners. This leads to passive aggressive behavior, pouting, moping, broken lines of communication, the carrying of grudges, and a whole host of other childish behaviors. Sadly, in the end, they mostly hurt themselves. Their lives are a long, sorry tale of broken relationships and fractured friendships. As the saying goes, bitterness is a poison pill one ingests while hoping to hurt the other person.

The benefit-of-the-doubters, on the other hand, are disarming. The more you hang around them the more comfortable you feel. You become less and less self-conscious, less afraid of being authentic, and less fearful of making mistakes. You begin to realize that even if you do mess up, you will likely be given the benefit-of-the-doubt and everything will be okay anyway. As a matter of fact, when you dig deep enough into the thought process of a benefit-of-the-doubter, you realize that they assign motives, too. It's just that they tend to assign positive ones to you instead of negative ones! Talk about "nice!" Who wouldn't want to hang around someone who was quick to think the best of us as a knee-jerk reaction to any of our actions?

As you consider these two types of people, I imagine you've already had names pop into your head of those who fit each of the categories. I know, it's hard not to do. But classifying people that way is almost as bad as assigning impure motives to their behavior! So stop it (and I will try to stop, as well!). Instead, take the constructive side of this message and analyze your own behavior. Are you a motive-assigner or a benefit-of-the-doubter? What would your five closest friends and/or family members have to say about you?

It's worth considering. And if you don't like the answer you get back about yourself, change!

If you don't? Well, it simply means that you are a lousy no-good loser that assigns motives to people because you've got an axe to grind with a chip on your shoulder about that one time you asked me . . . aw, never mind. I know why you did what you did, and I'm not speaking to you anymore.

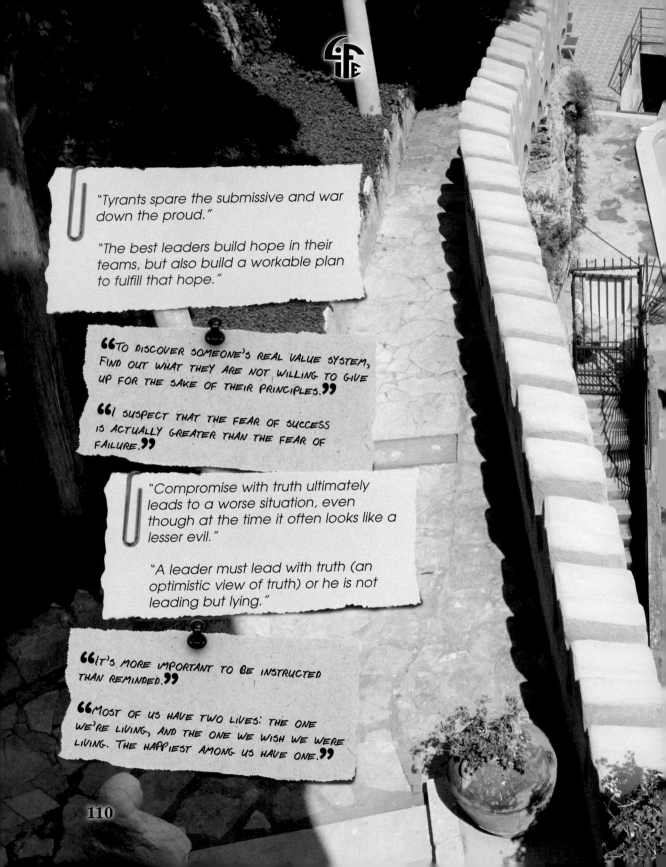

"Tyrants spare the submissive and war down the proud."

"The best leaders build hope in their teams, but also build a workable plan to fulfill that hope."

66To discover someone's real value system, find out what they are not willing to give up for the sake of their principles.99

66I suspect that the fear of success is actually greater than the fear of failure.99

"Compromise with truth ultimately leads to a worse situation, even though at the time it often looks like a lesser evil."

"A leader must lead with truth (an optimistic view of truth) or he is not leading but lying."

66It's more important to be instructed than reminded.99

66Most of us have two lives: the one we're living, and the one we wish we were living. The happiest among us have one.99

LiFe

"YOUR SELF—DECEPTION IS VERY ANNOYING TO ME. I AM GLAD I DON'T HAVE ANY WHATSOEVER OF MY OWN."

"THE CONCEPT OF INEVITABLE HUMAN IMPROVEMENT THROUGH SOCIETAL ADVANCES IS TERRIBLY NAIVE."

"Unsolved problems on the inside of a person stop success more often than problems on the outside of a person."

"Effort gives significance to life. What are you striving for?"

111

Excellence Begets Excellence

"He is lucky," they say. "Had some good breaks," say others. "Yup, knew the right people." "Plus, he was at the right place at the right time." These are the excuses people make vocally about others who've succeeded. Worse, these are the thought processes people uncritically buy into when confronted with the high achievement of others. As they say, the worst excuse is the one you sell yourself.

Why is it that we are so quick to explain away extraordinary accomplishments? Why is our knee-jerk reaction to downplay peak performance as a quirk or bestowment reserved for the precious few? Perhaps we've learned incorrectly how things work. Maybe we haven't been properly educated in the game of success. It's possible we haven't thought through our assumptions deeply enough. Most likely, however, these incorrect responses to high achievement are rooted in the fact that the performance of others makes our own pale in comparison. We reach for an explanation that takes the pressure off ourselves and find one readily at hand in the popular culture around us. Mediocrity is worshipped; decadence masquerades as creativity; and lazy is the new cool. People who strive for high achievement and excellence are freaks or sell-outs.

Truth, however, is a pesky thing. It doesn't seem to give way to fads, laziness, popular culture, excuses, anger, or false doctrines. It stands tall through it all. And the truth about high achievement and success is that it occurs on purpose, by design, through the tremendous commitment and persistence of individuals who have chosen the harder path. In other words: high achievement is earned.

This is bad news for someone searching for an excuse or wanting to explain away their own lack of success. On the contrary, however, it should be liberating for the person who has a big dream! The formula is available to anyone, and here it is:

Hard Work x Smart Work (Practice) x Time = High Achievement and Significance

Notice that this equation has almost nothing to say about talent, connections, or breaks. These things may lend a hand regarding starting points, but have virtually nothing to do with finishing at the peak.

The first component, hard work, is an unavoidable component in success. It simply cannot be avoided or bypassed. The hard truth is that if one wants significant results, significant effort will be required. Curiously, however, this one isn't so hard for people to stomach. Everyone seems to know hard work is a big part of success. What gets missed is that working hard is not the end in and of itself; it must be paired with smart work. This is effort expended toward intentional and painstaking improvement. It is not easy,

The hard truth is that if one wants significant results, significant effort will be required.

rarely fun, and isn't productive until mixed with the final component of time. Time is the great amplifier. It takes inputs and multiplies them into something seemingly greater than the sum of the parts. Intentional, improvement-oriented actions compound over time. Conversely, bad choices also compound over time. What one does in the little moments shows up in big outcomes over time.

These three components explain the greatest achievements of mankind. They are the tools of the mature, reserved for individuals committed to maximizing their gifts and making a difference in this world. They are best utilized by an adherence to the principles of excellence in thought and deed.

So now we have come full circle. Excellence results from excellence. Excellent outcomes come from excellent inputs. Excellence in practice, preparation, commitment, effort, attitude, relationships, goal setting, execution, measurement, analysis, improvement, and persistence produces excellence in results.

Are you dreaming of excellent outcomes in your life, career, business, marriage, home, church, or art?

Then do the hard work of adhering to the principles of excellence in everything you do. Raise your standards. Make excellence the cornerstone of the life you are constructing. Put it at the center of your personal culture. And don't worry about the competition. If you truly focus upon excellence, there won't be much competition.

LIFE

"All people experience failures in life. The successful people learn from them; the unsuccessful people quit them."

"Some people say they have to see it to believe it, but leaders have to believe it to see it."

"GOOD LEADERS HAVE INFLUENCE BECAUSE THEY HAVE CHARACTER, GET RESULTS, SHARE CREDIT, AND ACCEPT BLAME."

"GOOD LEADERS HAVE INFLUENCE BECAUSE OTHERS GET CAUGHT UP IN THEIR CAUSE."

"Success is pictured by the mind metaphysically before it is accomplished by the leader's efforts physically."

"When you decide to be a 5%er, 95% of the people will disagree with your choices."

GOOD LEADERS HAVE INFLUENCE BECAUSE PEOPLE GET CAUGHT UP IN THEIR VISION.

GOOD LEADERS HAVE INFLUENCE BECAUSE OTHERS BUY INTO THEM AS A PERSON.

Genteel Back-Channelers

Teams are endlessly interesting because they are made up of people. People, as we will learn throughout our lives, are mind-bogglingly complex. First of all, we get to deal with the two genders. Then we get to deal with those who are single and those who are wed, those who've been widowed and those who've been divorced, those who have children and those who do not. Then we find that people come from different cultures, speak different languages, and worship in different ways. We also discover that there are personality types or temperaments. Additionally, we are told that there are various natural "love languages." Then there are the youth and the elderly and the rest of us in between. Also, there are those who like the New England Patriots, and those who don't. But there is one more variation among individuals that I find worthy of mention, and it is this: how they behave when dealing with others.

Working with other people takes a special skill. It requires emotional maturity, patience, acceptance of others and their views, flexibility, the ability to listen, a certain degree of humility, the ability to influence, and the need from time to time to apologize. Some people tend to get pushed to the side in group settings, while others tend to do the pushing. Interactions vary according the an infinite number of combinations of the factors described in the first paragraph above. But there is one tendency, call it a trait, if you will, that is supremely destructive to human interaction and certainly to the functioning of a team. Some call it "Passive Aggressive" behavior, but when one reads the clinical definitions and professional opinions associated with that term, it doesn't quite fit what I'm discussing here. Nope. For our needs, we'll need to invent a new term. Let's call it:

GENTEEL BACK-CHANNELING

Just what exactly is "Genteel Back-Channeling?" It's the behavior of a person who is genteel in public but acidic in private. He or she will not confront the person with whom there is a problem, but will tell others all about it later. Genteel Back-Channelers are masters at involving those who are not part of the problem nor part of the solution. They expand the circle, so to speak, amplifying the problem. They throw gasoline on a spark instead of water. This type of person is conflict-averse and gossip-prone. He or she won't handle issues head-on and out in the open, but rather will "back channel," by trying to build up a coalition of people who "side with their view" through whispering campaigns in the shadows of the hallways. These people are political in nature: they play games and keep score. They generally get their feelings hurt, carry grudges, pout, and assign motives to the behavior of others. Genteel Back-Channelers can make the best of first-impressions but are usually marked by a trail of relational wrecks behind them.

How can you spot this behavior? Here are some signs:

1. "Hey, can I speak to you after the meeting?"
2. "I didn't want to say this in there, but, . . ."
3. "Do you agree with what Bob said? I'm not so sure . . ."
4. "Can you keep a secret?"
5. "I love Bob to death, but . . ."
6. "I didn't tell Bob this, but . . ."
7. "Bob's a great guy, has some great qualities, it's just that . . ."
8. "I don't think Bob knows how the rest of us are feeling . . ."
9. The "silent treatment"
10. Acting like nothing is wrong in public when they've said negative things in private.

It is important to understand this type of behavior because Genteel Back-Channelers appear nearly everywhere groups of people work together. Rare is the team or organization that doesn't have at least one in a position of influence. To have a highly functional team, however, Genteel Back-Channeling cannot be allowed. Otherwise, factions will develop, relationships will be damaged, political games will be played, and what happens "behind the scenes" will trump anything that happens out in the open.

So what do you do if your organization, team, work group, or (swallow hard) family has someone or several someones demonstrating Genteel Back-Channeling behavior?

1. Confront the situation head on, in love.
2. Give clear guidelines for acceptable behavior, but also for those which will not be tolerated. Make sure the whole team understands what's expected.
3. Pray for the offending individual, and for a sweet spirit in yourself as you deal with him or her.
4. If destructive behavior persists, remove the individual from the team or group. This will often be difficult, but entirely necessary. A dysfunctional team is no team at all. In some cases, you will simply have to disassociate with the person.
5. Check yourself against this kind of behavior and make sure your own example is beyond reproach. If it hasn't been, apologize and seek forgiveness.

If you have ever had the great fortune of working on a highly functioning team of people, you will know there are very few situations more fun and exciting, or more productive. But such a special situation can be utterly ruined by one person with that dangerous blend of pride and cowardice: the Genteel Back-Channeler. Like a little bit of arsenic in a batch of brownies, it doesn't take much to ruin the chemistry of a team.

There. You can't say you haven't been warned. (Just don't tell anyone who told you. It's just a secret between you and me. I love those other people to death, but . . .)

> "Busyness and idleness are two sides of the same coin: disorder. True rest is not idleness, but restoration."

> "Worry is the process of trying to fix things that haven't broken yet."

"Leaders help spread truth along without encumbering it with themselves."

"Winners think like winners even when they are losing."

EXCUSES ARE USELESS, EXCEPT FOR PREVENTING SUCCESS.

OPTIMISM IS UNDER-RATED IN THE ARENA OF ACHIEVEMENT.

119

"Are you a slave to money or is money your slave?"

"A leader should focus on giving more than he receives in each relationship."

GOOD LEADERS HAVE INFLUENCE BECAUSE PEOPLE WANT TO FOLLOW THEM.

THE FREEDOM TO DO WHAT ONE WANTS TO DO (IS CALLED TO DO) PROFESSIONALLY OR VOCATIONALLY IS A BLESSING INDEED.

"When your subconscious mind sees it, your conscious mind does it, and you get it."

"If you make it your practice to lift up others, they will make it their practice to lift up you, creating a win-win culture."

WHILE WE CAN CERTAINLY NEVER KNOW IT ALL, WE CAN AT LEAST LEARN WHAT WE NEED TO KNOW TO SUCCEED.

WHEN IT COMES TO BOOKING APPOINTMENTS, MAKE SURE IT'S SOLID. A LOOSE APPOINTMENT IS NO APPOINTMENT.

120

Proper Care and Feeding of Elephants

True achievers **visualize successful outcomes before making them a reality**. Athletes, salespeople, musicians, business owners and others understand the power of vision. The ability of the subconscious mind to lead someone towards his or her dominating vision is little known and rarely tapped into among the masses. For success, learning to feed the subconscious mind the vision of the future isn't a nice add-on: it's an absolute necessity. World-class athlete and author Vince Poscente wrote about the difference between the conscious and subconscious mind in his book, *The Ant and the Elephant*. He states that in one second of thinking through words the conscious mind stimulates two thousand neurons, while in one second of imagining through images the subconscious mind stimulates *four billion neurons*. That's literally two million *times* more neurons stimulated in the subconscious mind than the conscious mind in just *one second* of activity! Poscente called the conscious mind, "the ant" and the subconscious mind, "the elephant." Albert Einstein said, "Imagination is more important than knowledge." These concepts are not new, just unfortunately rarely applied.

> *Most men lead lives of quiet desperation.*
> – Henry David Thoreau

Henry David Thoreau, believing few ever accomplished what they dreamt, wrote, "Most men lead lives of quiet desperation." Sadly, his is a true picture of most lives, but it doesn't have to be. Changing one critical habit can make all the difference. Feeding the elephant is the key.

I (Orrin) like to imagine the bridling or disciplining of one's elephant as controlling the input to subconscious thought. We could call this controlling the elephant's food. Next, the elephant needs to be aligned with the logical thoughts of the conscious mind, or the ant. If the elephant and the ant are moving in the same direction, the ant can hop on the back of the elephant and ride to success. But if not aligned, there is a civil war in the brain that leads to indecision and inaction.

Perhaps a silly illustration will drive the point home. If one were to head into the jungle having an ant and an elephant as resources from which to choose, no one would hop on the back of the ant as the transportation of choice. Leaving the elephant behind while expecting the ant to do the carrying would be backbreaking for the ant and miserable for the rider. A better plan would be to choose the elephant, then feed him properly for the journey. This "feeding" would likely involve conjuring an image of a distant oasis, exciting the elephant to charge ahead, thereby encouraging him to carry the ant and rider all the way to success.

This analogy represents a logical plan to utilize the whole brain to achieve life goals, not merely the conscious and logical thinking part of the brain. In real application this technique will still take work, effort and drive to achieve, but by lining up the ant and the elephant, the mind's civil war is ended, and the conditions for massive success have been created. It is neither a person's starting conditions, nor outside circumstances, but this civil war inside the mind that short-circuits achievement. Feeding the ant *and* the elephant is definitely an inside job; igniting the elephant with an image of a brighter tomorrow can end the civil war. Proper feeding ends the time wasted and the frustration experienced by riding the ant.

If one will not feed his or her elephant, someone or something else will.

One additional thought regarding the care and feeding of elephants is that they refuse to starve. This means if one will not feed his or her elephant, someone or something else will. Consider our modern media and the firestorm of images we continuously have forced upon us. Every product's advertisement is geared toward the elephant. Commercials do not give lists of functions, features and benefits to the ant, but instead they feed elephants with attractive images of the success to be garnered by using their products. Advertisements speak right past the ants and instead feed the elephants by creating needs through repetition of mesmerizing images over and over. As a result of this, people will often buy things they don't really need without ever understanding the influence behind their actions. Remember: people make decisions emotionally (through the power of the elephant) and then explain it rationally (with the logic of the ant).

As a kid I loved watching any televised sport whenever I was able. I must have seen thousands of beer commercials over the course of those years. "Tastes Great - Less Filling," and other slogans are still in my head even though I haven't seen those commercials in a very long time. All beer advertisements are fed to the elephant, not the ant. Imagine an advertisement for beer in which the ratio of carbonated water to barley and hops is explained in intricate detail. An "ant" version of a beer advertisement would explain how alcohol blocks oxygen from the brain, thereby causing impaired thinking and motor skills. Instead, beer advertisements implant images that feed our elephants. They flash video clips of a guy opening a beer can, and then suddenly, like magic, bikini-clad women appear all around him. Rationally, men know this isn't reality (at least for most of us), but the elephant has received its marching instructions and charges out to buy beer any way. People may initially resist the influence, but through constant exposure that feeds the elephant bit by bit, eventually the elephant runs toward the vision. If it weren't an effective technique, it isn't likely that advertising executives would continue to pay big money to run their commercials. I remember the day that I began a habit based on such commercials: after finishing an intramural basketball game, I headed to the bar with the guys for a "cold one." It wasn't until years afterward I realized someone had programmed my elephant and I was acting accordingly.

The fact is, an elephant will charge. The only question is, who will give it its direction? Make sure your elephant is fed, and fed only the best food! Welcome to the jungle.

SUCCESS IS AVAILABLE WHEN YOU DECIDE TO DISCIPLINE YOUR ELEPHANT WITH YOUR DREAMS AS MUCH AS YOU DISCIPLINE YOUR ANT WITH YOUR RESPONSIBILITIES.

"Winners manage frustration while losers succumb to it."

"People forgive a leader's skill deficiency much more quickly than they will forgive character deficiency."

"WHAT YOU DO DAILY IS PART OF WHAT YOU BECOME PERMANENTLY."

"TRUE WEALTH LIES IN DISCOVERING HOW LITTLE YOU CAN BE HAPPY WITH."

"Many know what to do, but winners do what they know."

"Success breeds more success until it breeds pride, forgetfulness, and finally failure."

"LIFE HINGES ON DEFINING MOMENTS. HOW WE BEHAVE IN THOSE MOMENTS REFLECTS WHAT WE WERE DOING BEFORE THE PRESSURE WAS ON."

"The majority of the people are failing financially, because they follow the advice of the majority of the people."

"We can learn more from the errors of great thinkers than the accuracies of ordinary minds."

The Lesson of the Double Jump

In my crazy teenage years I (Chris) became consumed by a magnificent obsession. It was on my mind in the morning, afternoon, evening, and night. As my tee shirt at the time said: I ate, drank, slept, walked, talked, breathed, and lived motorcycles; specifically, motocross.

This was a little before the X-game craze; back when riding a motocross bike meant speed around a track more than tricks in the air. Still, the obstacles of a typical course were challenging and required all sorts of aerial maneuvers for effective racing. Chief among these was something called the "double jump" (and its cousin, the "triple jump," operating in much the same way).

The concept is simple. Two jumps are placed a significant distance apart. The fastest way to negotiate that part of the track is to hit the first jump and clear the second one, ideally landing on its down slope. This is called "doubling." Wherever a double jump existed on a track, to be among the fastest riders and therefore have a chance of claiming the trophy, bragging rights, and adoration of "pit tootsies," one had to "double." To hit both jumps individually was slow and downright embarrassing. There is nothing like having all the endorphins a teenager can muster in motion, while controlling a highly tuned racing machine only to have another such teenager fly past you in the air. The thought of it can still keep me awake at night. Besides, doubling meant flying much higher and farther through the air, and heck, that was worth it all by itself.

So we (my buddies and I) had to learn to double. We literally dug into the project. Every day after school we'd grab our shovels and head out to our make-shift practice track behind the Johnsons' house across the street. Spade-full after spade-full we'd hurl, until eventually we had constructed a pretty fair replica of what we were seeing on the official tracks on the weekends.

And of course, we all raced to be the first to try it out.

Everything is different the first time you approach a double jump. It's the same terrain leading up to it, but the whole time, you are aware of the challenge on the horizon. Somewhere in the far reaches of your mind, the task ahead looms largely like a heavy cloud over the rest of the track. It doesn't help that your buddies are usually watching, too, ready to laugh, point, jibe, or call an ambulance, in whatever combination they feel appropriate. Finally, the jump is just around the next corner. You fumble your way through it, making the worst turn through that section ever. The nerves are building. The tingle in your throat is there. Your heart is beating hard in your chest. Your breathing slows into shallow little flutters. And then you reach it: the point of no return. It's that moment when you either goose the throttle all the way in total commitment or wimp out and back off, desperately searching for a plausible excuse for your cowardice. It's in that moment when you find out what you're made of, when you learn if you've got what it takes to push yourself beyond the limit, when you discover if you have courage. Your boldness (or lack thereof) is now public, your lunacy confirmed or denied. And usually, you clear the thing by twenty feet!

"That wasn't so bad!" is the normal response. The hardest part was truly deciding to do it; to wick that throttle all the way at that critical moment of no return and hang on for dear life.

Following a successful jump, you are then qualified to 'encourage' the others to do it, too, with helpful rejoinders such as "Come on, you sissies, it was nothing!"

Sometimes, however, the story goes a little differently. In the moment where it counts, where there is no turning back, where one must fully commit to jumping the double, some hesitate, back off, or chicken out. Usually this occurs when it is officially too late to turn back, when speed is too high to safely hit each jump individually but not high enough to actually clear the second one. The result is not pretty. The term for it is "casing" the second jump. Normally, when a rider reduces throttle suddenly in a panic and hits the first jump, the back of the motorcycle rises up menacingly while the front sinks like a stone. This combination – while at the same time hurling through the air at the face of the second jump – is enough to scare anyone out of his wits. It is also enough to cause serious bodily harm. Look through any collection of YouTube videos of this event to see what I mean. It is calamitous, and it was entirely caused by the hesitation of the rider. In most cases, if he (or she) had just stayed with his commitment to clear the double and not backed off or hesitated, he would have been fine. But logic is a little chicken when fear comes around.

This little lesson in motocross dynamics is more than just a stroll down Memory Lane, it's a metaphor for life. As we live out our days, we will be confronted with many figurative "double jumps." What had been normal before will be changed by some event or opportunity on the horizon. Mustering the boldness, courage, fortitude and guts to hurl ourselves over the obstacle will usually result in all sorts of rewards and self-satisfaction. Failing to handle it so well will likely result in damage, loss, and

As we live out our days, we will be confronted with many figurative "double jumps."

regret. The result is up to us. And usually, it all comes down to our response in that one small moment of decision.

Will we have the guts to do the right thing? To stand our ground? To accelerate when most sane people would say to slow down? To push for great when good is so enticing? To serve others even when it hurts? To try our hardest when others are loafing? To push through the fears at the edge of our comfort zone and go into new territory? To force ourselves to fly higher and farther than ever before? To face up to ourselves in ways that show us what we're truly made of? To find out if we've got what it takes? To learn once and for all if we have courage or are a coward?

> Perhaps most people don't want to face up to these hard moments in life.

Perhaps most people don't want to face up to these hard moments in life. Perhaps they don't really want to learn what's inside because they think they might not like what they'll see. That's understandable. But just like that bunch of Michigan teenagers in a vacant field in the nineteen-eighties, you won't know until you try. And I personally believe that you'll like the feeling of pushing past your comfort zone and confronting your fears, even if you crash and burn a few times. Eventually, with enough attempts, with enough bold decisions in the face of fear, you'll discover just how far and how high you can fly.

PREPARE TO SURPRISE YOURSELF!

"Societies, Civilizations & Corporations all decay from within before they are overcome from without."

"Success is hidden inside of hard work; that is why so many never find it."

WE MUST BE DIFFERENT TO MAKE A DIFFERENCE IN THE WORLD.

IN OUR WORLD, INGRATITUDE IS DISGUISED AS VICTIMIZATION, AND CYNICISM AS INTELLIGENCE.

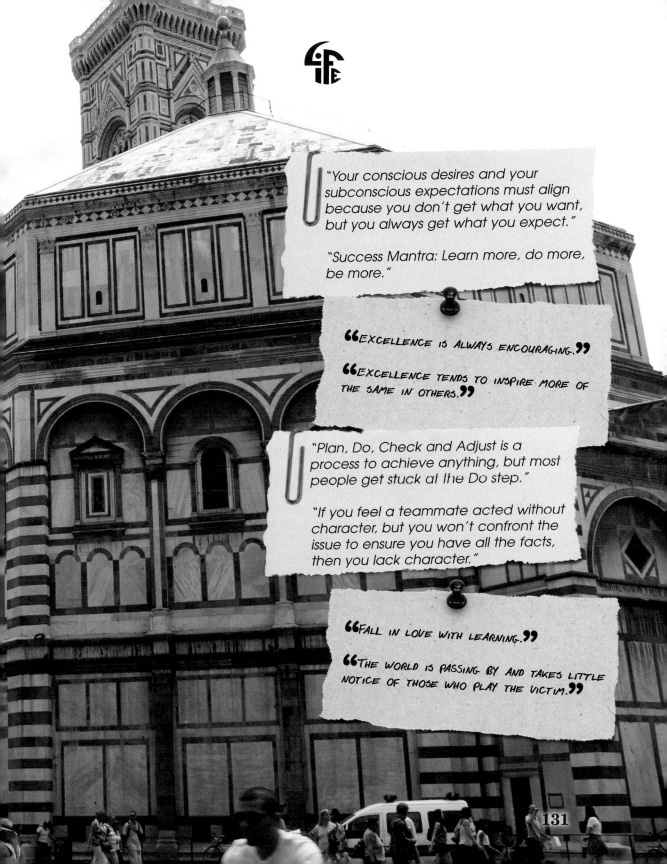

"Your conscious desires and your subconscious expectations must align because you don't get what you want, but you always get what you expect."

"Success Mantra: Learn more, do more, be more."

"EXCELLENCE IS ALWAYS ENCOURAGING."

"EXCELLENCE TENDS TO INSPIRE MORE OF THE SAME IN OTHERS."

"Plan, Do, Check and Adjust is a process to achieve anything, but most people get stuck at the Do step."

"If you feel a teammate acted without character, but you won't confront the issue to ensure you have all the facts, then you lack character."

"FALL IN LOVE WITH LEARNING."

"THE WORLD IS PASSING BY AND TAKES LITTLE NOTICE OF THOSE WHO PLAY THE VICTIM."

131

The Camel's Nose Under the Tent Flap

People don't like to be told what to do. Even children are not very receptive to instruction. So when governments set out to take over peoples' freedoms (which means, quite simply, government telling people what to do instead of people making their own choices) they have to get crafty. Some serious skill is required. That's where politicians come in. Politicians are educated in the arts of "creep." Not to be confused with the derogatory word which, coincidentally, can accurately be applied to many bureaucrats, "creep" is a term used to describe a specific strategy nearly perfected by governments. Here's how it works:

Since people don't like to be told what to do and will generally resist being bossed around, something must happen to convince them to allow what would normally and naturally be considered contrary to their best interest. Although there are many ways to get the process started, usually a crisis of some sort is extremely useful. As one politician recently slipped up and stated publicly, "Never waste a good crisis." A crisis causes fear. Fear inhibits clear thinking and causes all kinds of knee-jerk reactions. One such reaction is to allow people in power to utilize that power to "do something." Almost always, that "doing something" involves the growth of government through the creation of new agencies, bureaus, boards, committees, programs, expenditures, and the passing of new laws. This would all be fine and dandy, except for three little reasons:

Fear inhibits clear thinking and causes all kinds of knee-jerk reactions.

1. They cost money and therefore create massive problems of their own,
2. They generally don't work, and finally,
3. They generate secondary consequences (some would say "unintended" consequences, but given the power lust of many bureaucrats, one wonders).

With each new government creation the "creep" into our personal freedoms increases.

Freedom shrinks as governmental interference grows.

Many think it's all okay as long as they are getting their pet programs, handouts, freebies, kickbacks, and power perks. This is why a growing "mooching class" always accompanies a growing government. As this plays out, "experts" in government get to decide things we ought to be free to decide for ourselves. "They" are cock-sure that they know what is better for us than we do. Programs and "Great Societies" and "fairer resource management" and "progress" are trumpeted as grand new foolproof ideas. But it is really the same old story of control over the many, by the privileged few, that litters the pages of every history book. Freedom bleeds to death on the altar of government worship.

There is a cute illustration often used to describe creep, and it goes like this: Anyone who has ever spent any time around animals knows they are filthy. Camels, famously, are some of the nastiest and filthiest of all. Traveling in caravans across the sub-Saharan deserts for centuries, traders would tie up their camels a distance far enough from their tent to prevent the camels from trying to get in. Nobody, no matter how dependent upon his camel for survival and transportation, would choose to lodge alongside his camel inside the warmth and comfort of his own tent. The camels, however, resisted this fact. No matter how unwanted they were within the confines of their owner's tent, they still desired to partake in a little of that luxury themselves. They would start their attempt by pushing only their nose under the tent flap. If this went successfully unnoticed, they would slide the full length of their head in. Gradually, little by little, they would stick their whole neck inside, and finally their whole body. Suddenly, it would seem, the whole animal would be entirely inside the tent enjoying the shelter from the elements, crowding out the tent's rightful owner. Government can be seen to act in the same way. "It's just a temporary expedient until the crisis is abated," they say, sliding their nose under the flap. "Just a little while longer and we'll have this problem licked," they say, sliding in their entire head and neck. And on it goes. As President Reagan said, "There is nothing quite so permanent as a temporary government program."

The strangest fact, however, is that so many people seem intent on actually *helping* the camel sneak into the tent! But a little thought is all that's required to explain this strange situation: they don't want a camel in their *own* tent; they only want to help one get into *yours!* However, if they really have bought so far into the blind dribble of our day to actually think they want a camel in their own tent, then, well, I suppose they deserve the flea bites they'll receive.

> *Freedom bleeds to death on the altar of government worship.*

Leaders Make Right Choices

Character demands strength of mind, heart, and will. Choosing to do right, regardless of what others are doing, isn't easy or natural. Leaders refuse to surrender their character, considering it more valuable than any earthly possession. Many talk glibly of character, boasting loudly of its importance, but when circumstances press against them, they quickly run to the easier wrong rather than the more difficult right. Character is less about head-knowledge of knowing right or wrong, but more about heart-knowledge - doing right even when it hurts. In life, one can choose to produce results or search for ways to exploit others' results. Producers create value by serving people, either directly in fields of service, or indirectly by producing products for people. Producers do not look for handouts – only "hand ups." Given the right training, producers can achieve nearly anything with effort and tenacity. Maintaining a productive existence requires character, however, since exploiting someone else's results is tempting and seems easier. But people will not remain in business with exploiters unless coerced. One of the quickest ways to recognize producers is by the long-term relationships they have built through serving others.

One of the quickest ways to recognize producers, is by the long-term relationships built through serving others through win-win principles.

Exploiters, on the other hand, produce nothing, relying on privileged positions gained through their political maneuverings. Exploiters seek out producers, needing production in order to live their parasitic existences, hoping to fatten themselves from the fruits grown in others' gardens. Some fields are ripe for exploitation, because they allow employees to remain far removed from the customer's satisfaction. Exploiters can be found in any profession where someone has discovered how to gain at another's expense without serving.

Free enterprise works because the customer is sovereign over his personal wishes. If a consumer's choices are forced, he has lost his freedom to choose, and without economic freedom, there is no true freedom at all. In free enterprise, if customers aren't happy, they find someone else to meet their needs. Freedom ensures that money is made through service to customers,

Freedom ensures that money is made through service to customers, not by control over them.

not by control over them. Supporting Free Enterprise takes character, because it gives power to the consumers, not to the State or Big Business. Any alternate economic system denies the consumer rights, leaving someone else as the final arbiter of the customers' wishes, making a mockery of freedom. If all businesses were free from government partnership, exploiters would be forced to serve the customers, so the companies would either change or go out of business. Free Enterprise, by making the customer king, ensures that all businesses are created to serve customers.

In contrast, much that is written on the alleged benefits of socialism, a sad economic system debunked in theory, (see Ludwig Von Mises), and in practice, (see everywhere it has been attempted), has been written by exploiters, seeking a place to hide from their personal and professional incompetence. Why would any exploiter write anything truthful about a system assured to deny him that privileged and unearned position? Instead, exploiters will blather about equality and fairness, without defining the terms, making the confused customer forget that true freedom would make him sovereign over his own choices. I am reminded of a famous quote often credited to Winston Churchill which says, "If you aren't socialist before twenty-five, you have no heart; if you are socialist after twenty-five, you have no brain." Sadly, in our society, many are losing their brains, with producers being attacked by a growing legion of exploiters, not truly because production is wrong, but simply that exploiters want more of the producers' production. Socialism is an acid; it decays the roots of our freedoms, feeds the worst aspects of human nature, and gives pride, greed and envy free reign to destroy. Is this the future to which we look forward in this once great nation?

> *If you aren't socialist before twenty-five, you have no heart; if you are socialist after twenty-five, you have no brain.*

LET EVERYONE EXAMINE HIMSELF.

This leads us full circle in our discussion; leaders must choose right. America, like other countries, stands or falls based on the amount of producers compared to exploiters in

society. The more exploitation is rewarded, the more difficult it is to be a producer.
History teaches that when a country develops more exploiters than producers, that
country falls. There is hope, because many leaders are developing who are unwilling to
surrender this nation to exploiters. Just because it would be easier to become a member of
the thriving exploiters' community known simply as the, "Something For Nothing Club,"
(SFNC), doesn't mean it is right. One person of character standing on principle produces
more than a thousand who have surrendered their character to the SFNC. Be a producer
in life. Make choices based on character instead of convenience.

PERHAPS YOUR CHOICE WILL BE THE TIPPING POINT THAT MAKES ALL THE DIFFERENCE.

"Leaders must change the facts by confronting their weaknesses to turn them into strengths."

"Licking your wounds will not stop the bleeding, but applying pressure will."

"There are no regrets for a life lived leading."

"Calling them 'political parties' is a misnomer. They are more like 'wakes' than parties."

"Many times leaders are throwing people life jackets instead of letting God teach them to swim."

"Competition keeps you from buying your own excuses."

"Rascals ignore the tyranny of 'they.'"

"Rascals don't live their lives seeking the approval of others. They respond to their own inner voice."

137

"Uncommon courage is what separates good leaders from great leaders."

"You get what you believe. Change your belief window & you change your results."

Rainy people are those who always throw a cloud over good humor, good moods, and good times. Sad for them.

The passive life is not worth living. Get up and get going.

"While many are saying that it can't be done; leaders are getting it done."

"Leadership boils down to the two things that most people cannot resist, love and service."

When you get kicked, get down, and get depressed, massive action and service to others is the road out.

Meet people where they are, but help them to become the best they can be.

"Working hard without a dream is like rowing a boat in the middle of the ocean without knowing the way to shore."

"People naturally love competition & avoid confrontation, but true leadership requires cooperation & confrontation."

66 LEARNING IS ONE OF LIFE'S BIGGEST BLESSINGS. 99

66 TACKLE THE DIFFICULT THINGS FIRST. 99

But God

Days begin, bright and clean,
Little is known, most just shown.
We don't remember, maybe none can,
When we first realized something is wrong.
But God . . .
A confine from which memory cannot serve.
But all of us know it now, though some deny,
The crack, the void, the dark, the wound,
The thorn in the flesh, the plank in the eye.
But God . . .
Its presence grows, its power expands,
Splitting foundations of rock to sand.
Time assists in its creeping way,
The shadowy hand on our loss of days.
But God . . .
We mourn too, for our earlier selves,
All the while losing cheer to the truth.
Mirth dies on its edge, bleeding a helpless dirge,
A blight on light, hope, and love.
But God . . .
The core is black, the pit is deep,
Haunting even children in sleep.
What was beautiful takes a tarnish,
As all things human bear its stamp.
But God . . .
A cursed people, a fallen race,
From Adam's apple to dust in a grave,
Pinned to the ground, and stapled down,
Held back, restrained, kept in pain.
But God . . .
The trap is shut, the pincers close,
The prey fights in futile struggle.

But God.

Ephesians 2:4-5

LIFE

"Don't run from problems, because wherever you go, there you are."

"If you work hard, you make a living. If you work hard on yourself, you make a fortune."

"SHIN: A DEVICE FOR FINDING FURNITURE IN THE DARK."

"I USED TO EAT A LOT OF NATURAL FOODS UNTIL I LEARNED THAT MOST PEOPLE DIE OF NATURAL CAUSES."

LEADERSHIP: CONTROL AND INFLUENCE

D on't let the issues outside of your control stop you from addressing issues inside of your control.

If we have seen it once we have seen it a thousand times: a talented person with a willingness to work stopped cold by dwelling on issues outside of his or her control. This type of thinking takes many forms. Let us give you an example to help you recognize it in your own thinking. Suppose you are considering attending a certain school. Upon learning that one of your friends attended the school, you seek him out to learn from his experiences. If he shares that he quit the school because it was too hard and required too many hours of study and not enough for play, that doesn't mean you shouldn't attend. If you have a dream, and are willing to work, your friend's experience doesn't tell you anything about your potential at the school, since education, like nearly all of life, is a matter of personal responsibility. However, if your friend's failed attempt at school blocks your dream to even apply, then two failures have occurred: one-a failure of action, the other-a failure of thinking. How do you control your friend's work ethic? How do you know if your friend was truly committed to the school and his dreams? Why are you letting your friend's actions hinder your opportunities? **Leaders can only control themselves and the decisions they make,** while with others they have only influence and not control.

There are numerous examples of poor thinking in allowing issues outside of your control to affect the issues inside of your control. Here are some other poor thinking scenarios, each with a counter-point of more productive thinking:

1. I don't attend church because a hypocrite goes there. (Why allow a hypocrite to stop you from learning Truth for you and your family?)
2. I am not a business owner because I had a bad experience with a business person. (Why allow a bad business person to deny you a future of opportunities?)
3. I don't go to doctors because I had a bad experience with a doctor. (Why threaten your health because of one doctor's incompetence?)
4. I don't read because a teacher told me that I was dyslexic and would never be able to read. (Why allow a teacher's label to halt your personal growth?)
5. I don't talk to people because my parents told me that I was shy. (Why allow your parents' label from childhood hinder you as an adult?)

6. I don't attempt great things for God because my family has never accomplished anything great. (Why allow your family's past to hinder your future?)
7. I don't save money because I was told that I would always be in debt. (Why allow someone's poor thinking on money to become your thinking?)
8. I don't dream because I saw my friend dream and fail. (Why not learn from failures instead of becoming one?)
9. I am not getting married because so many people get divorces. (Why not learn from the successful marriages instead of focusing on the failed ones?)
10. I am not having children because the world is so messed up. (Why not learn how to prepare children for life versus denying them the opportunity for life?)

We could go on and on, but are quite sure the point is clear. Instead of allowing the things that you don't control (other people's thoughts and actions) to create your reality, why not focus upon the things you do control (your own thoughts and actions)?

Orrin Wooward grew up in Columbiaville, Michigan, a small village with few, if any big thinkers. It would have been easy to succumb to the "stinking thinking" of this environment, but through God's Grace, and with a ton of effort, he broke free from the mold. Instead of dwelling on his parents' faults, he focused on his parents' strengths. He learned from them a work ethic and the ability to think, and applied these to every endeavor he undertook.

One of the keys to breaking out is to **major on your majors,** not on the failed minors of others. Yes, people will let you down, shame on them, but that shouldn't stop you from fulfilling your purpose. Yes, your family may hurt you at times, but that doesn't end your responsibility to love and lead them. Yes your vision, like a ship, may take on water every now and then, but leaders understand that it's part of the journey to rebuild the ship bigger and stronger. **Your dream cannot be stolen, but through poor thinking, it can be surrendered.**

Life for that Orrin is much easier since he decided two things: 1) to press on regardless of the actions of others, and 2) that he was in the game no matter what. This released the stress and anxiety, felt by most people, when not truly committed to a course of action. Leaders make a decision, back that decision with full commitment, and make the decision right with overwhelming passion and effort.

We cannot control other people's poor decisions, but compounding the mistake by "piling on" is the last thing we should do. We have witnessed many people with more talent than we have sabotage their own success by allowing poor thinking to take root in their minds. Usually, by the time the weeds have ruined their thinking, they no longer are interested in hearing the advice necessary to help pull the weeds, and they sometimes even get offended at the suggestion that they are growing weeds.

Thus, one of the biggest weeds is permitting issues outside of your control to hinder your attitude and actions on the issues inside of your control. It truly is that simple, though not that easy.

Success in life is simply a matter of staying focused on the areas that you control while surrendering to God the areas that are outside of your control. What a leader eventually discovers is that others will be influenced by the leader's example, and they will address issues, and improve their performance; this is accomplished through the leader's influence, not as a result of his control. Communities of followers are not inspired to improve if the leader dwells upon areas outside of his control. It is only when the leader stays the course, even when it hurts, that others gain strength to resolve and change their own lives. The question to ask is: are you that type of leader for your family, community, and team?

One of the best decisions a leader will ever make in life is to be "all in," that is, fully committed to whatever field he is pursuing. Greatness doesn't happen to those who dabble, nor to those who deliberate, but only to those who decide. Pull the weeds from your thoughts.

TODAY IS THE DAY TO START THINKING LIKE THE LEADER YOU PLAN ON BECOMING.

"NOT ALL OF US DIE IN THE END. SOME DO IN THE MIDDLE."

"WE NEVER REALLY GROW UP. WE ONLY LEARN HOW TO ACT IN PUBLIC."

"Most people would rather live with comfortable lies than uncomfortable truths."

"To be ignorant of your ignorance is the greatest ignorance."

"TRUE CHAMPIONS DEAL IN THE CURRENCY OF PURPOSE. THEY TRADE THEIR TIME AND EFFORT FOR GREATER CONTRIBUTION.**"**

"Character is more important than reputation by magnitudes. Reputation is based upon others' opinions; character is based upon facts."

"DRIVEN BY THE PURPOSE FOR WHICH THEY WERE BORN, WINNERS AWAKE RUNNING THEIR RACE.**"**

"Priorities are you telling your time where it is going, instead of you asking where your time went."

"WE CAN NEVER BE PERFECT, BUT WE MUST NEVER CEASE WANTING TO BE.**"**

"If you are not willing to put in 100% until you see results, then you will never see results."

"An expert is sold on the old paradigm & unopen to new ideas while a student is always questioning & learning."

"WHO YOU ARE IS MORE IMPORTANT THAN WHAT YOU DO.**"**

"Talent to start is abundant; persistence to finish is rare."

"IGNORANCE HAS NO LIMITS.**"**

"Too often we view learning as a period of life, instead of a way of life."

Reading for Lifetime Growth

I picked up a book by Donald Trump because I had a strong desire to conquer the "money thing." The best I can remember, it was the first book after college I read on my own compulsion. I wish I could say that it sparked a hunger for lifetime learning, but alas, either Donald wasn't that compelling, or I wasn't ready, but it accomplished nothing. Next I remember reading part of a book on US Presidents and their secret wars. Next came an insider's account of the Mafia. Broad, unfocused, and spanning at least a couple years, this reading was seasoned with a heavy dose of motorcycle magazines.

It wasn't that I couldn't read. It wasn't that I didn't like to read. It was just that nobody, anywhere, at any time during my six years and two degrees of education had ever gotten it through my skull (nor even tried, truth be told) that reading is one of the most important habits for lifetime growth. At best, I considered reading to be a pass-time, something one did on the beach, airplane, or at moments of boredom. At worst, I considered it a waste of time. What could possibly be beneficial about sitting around reading when one could be out doing?

Then my business association with Orrin Woodward began, and he and other leaders taught me the importance of a self-directed education. I learned that the right kind of reading isn't a pass-time, but rather one of the best routes to fulfilling our natural hunger for gaining understanding, insight, and perspective. I also learned that although passive in appearance, reading is one of the activities that most awakens the brain, thereby ultimately leading the person to action – the best kind of action – the kind controlled by clear thought. In effect, reading correctly and with a purpose becomes a strategic weapon in a competitive world. **Let's face it: we are living in the Information Age.** Without the right information properly applied, one cannot hope to compete. There will simply be too many others willing to do the work to learn what they need to know to excel instead. In short, one of the biggest secrets to high achievement in life is to make reading your weapon of preparation.

I could go on, but my goal here is not to convince you of all the advantages of reading. Instead, I'd like to draw a distinction for you: don't simply read – study. Here are some suggestions for making your reading much more effective:

> *One of the biggest secrets to high achievement in life is to make reading your weapon of preparation.*

1. Read the right kinds of books, with the specific intent of improving yourself as a person. You can (and probably should) read certain books just for their entertainment value. But these should be seasoning, sprinkled in among the more edifying works.
2. Read about both the principles and specifics in the area of your profession, vocation, or passion. (Blessed is the person who aligns all three.)
3. Read broadly across many genres. Allow me to recommend some categories: Leadership (of course), Success, Theology, History, Economics, the Classics, Politics and Freedom, Finances and Investing.
4. Be reading through several books at any given time. This keeps any one author's voice from becoming too tedious and extends the amount of time you can read and stay fresh and engaged.
5. Devour your books. Underline passages, make notes in the margin, summarize key thoughts, outline important points in the blank pages at the back, etc. In other words, make the book your own. Adding all these markings draws a deeper understanding as you read the book the first time, provides a succinct summary to review before putting the completed book back upon the shelf, and makes future reference much easier.

6. Ask yourself for each book read: What were the author's key points and how can I apply them to my life right now?
7. Write the date you begin reading a book inside the front cover.
8. Keep a journal that includes a list tracking the books you've read. Record the title, author, genre, and date you finished reading each book. This allows, in one glance, a quick indication of the size and scope of your reading.
9. Promote books to others and help people solve problems and improve their lives by directing them to the books that have provided answers you've found helpful.
10. Make reading a priority. Eliminate the "good" activities from your crowded schedule and make room for the "great."

If you love what you do, you'll never work another day in your life.

One may be tempted to think that such a list represents a lot of work. I would like to suggest that nothing could be further from the truth. As the saying goes, "If you love what you do, you'll never work another day in your life." What you will discover is that reading of this caliber becomes an enjoyable passion all its own. That's because it will apply directly to improving your thoughts, knowledge, and understanding. It will increase your prowess and attitude. It will inspire you to dig deeper into mysteries and areas totally dark to you previously. One great book will lead to another. One deep insight will lead to further break-through thoughts and distinctions. Reading to the point of study will become a habit for lifetime growth, and a sustainable advantage few will ever match.

Dig in. Start reading with a purpose. See
for yourself how it develops into a passion. Watch the progress you'll make in life. Not only will you be hooked – you'll be hooked up. You'll be joining the "great conversation" among the strongest thinkers, the deepest probers, and the loftiest dreamers of the human experience.

"When you argue for your limitations you perpetuate them."

"Never let your comforts overcome your convictions."

66Thinking is what matters most when it comes to succeeding.99

66Delay is the enemy of success.99

"It's not what you don't know that is holding you back as much as it's not doing what you do know. Do more and you will learn more!."

"When you aim for the stars, you must be prepared for some scars."

66Performance in the clutch reveals preparation in the quiet.99

66A penny saved is a government oversight.99

Leaders are Gardeners of Their Own Minds

It's amazing how much one can learn from a person just by listening. People who believe they have a positive attitude give away their negativity when they speak. We like to begin mentoring sessions with, "Tell me the good, the bad, and the ugly. The good we will celebrate, the bad we will adjust, and the ugly we will pray about." This is sure to get people talking, helping us to identify, not just what happened, but how they are thinking about what happened – which, in the end, is more important than the event, since the event happens only once, but how they think about the event repeats over and over in their minds and hearts.

Painful experiences happen to both achievers and non-achievers alike. The difference in outcomes is in their respective responses; achievers learn from the bad cards and choose to draw more, while non-achievers complain about the cards of life being stacked against them and choose to quit the game. In reality, what's actually stacked against them is their own thinking. Winners received the same stimulus, but chose to respond differently than the non-winners.

When something bad happens to a winner, he immediately focuses on minimizing its effects, learning anything he can from the situation: no pity parties, no 'woe is me' attitudes, just resolution and teachable moments. The extent to which a person wins in life is many times related to how quickly he can go from "problem identified" to "problem solved," all the while learning through the pain of the process. When a person's attitude stays down for weeks, months, or even sometimes years at a time, can a positive outcome be expected? There is only so much mental energy to go around. When this energy is spent dwelling on negative thoughts, allowing them to enter the heart, eventually pouring out of the mouth, why is anyone shocked that so little is accomplished in life? The key is pulling the weeds (negative thoughts) when they are first detected entering the mind. Weeds are much easier to pull when immediately seized, but much tougher when allowed to root in the heart. By the time the weeds of negative thinking have taken root to the point of affecting our speech, we know that they've grown strong and deep.

Leaders are gardeners of their own minds, identifying and pulling weeds quickly.

Leaders are gardeners of their own minds, identifying and pulling weeds quickly. The best leaders appear never to be down attitudinally, because they choose to pull weeds promptly. But if they ever are down, they certainly don't spread the disease to others. This is because great leaders understand the power of their own example, and understand that the maintenance of this example is their responsibility. This is not to say that leaders work entirely alone. If a weed is extra difficult, the best leaders have the discipline to seek out mentors for help, thereby refusing to contaminate

150

others with even the toughest of weeds. It can be seen, then, that one of the first and most important assignments of any would-be leader is consistent and prompt pulling of his weeds. It's not an option if he plans on inspiring others, since a bitter attitude and sour face inspire no one.

To become a great leader, pull your weeds, guard your mind, and protect your heart, for out of the abundance of the heart the mouth speaks. Leadership occurs when people have confidence in the leader. If a person's attitude is unpredictable or negative, he disqualifies himself for leadership, because this behavior only repels and causes doubt. Leaders are dealers in hope, change, and growth, all of which begin inside the leader himself.

LAUNCH A LEADERSHIP REVOLUTION IN YOUR OWN LIFE BY BECOMING A GOOD GARDENER OF YOUR OWN THOUGHTS.

"When you feel down, focus on all the things that you are thankful for in your life to maintain an attitude of gratitude."

"Setting a goal is invaluable. You gain either success or added experience in preparation for success."

66 The easiest way to find something lost around the house is to buy a replacement. 99

66 Greatness never happens by accident. 99

"One of a leader's main assignments is to impart belief into others that they are worthy of success."

"You start leading your life the moment you realize your ability to conquer both yourself and your environment."

66 People get emotional defending their opinion when they aren't very sure why they have it. 99

66 Leaders cannot be fainthearted. 99

"To make it as a political commentator one must have either big teeth or be good at interrupting (or both)."

"Leaders have to tear down fences. But they should also first find out why those fences were put there to begin with."

"If success were easy, everyone would be successful. Stop looking for easy & start looking for worthy of your best."

"If you don't do something different, you will end up where you are going."

153

Husband, Father, Leader: Play the Man

In today's society, young men wanting to learn character, responsibility, and leadership, are struggling to find role models to follow. The mainstream media seems to despise worthy role models – men who have the courage to lead in their families, businesses, and communities –instead believing this model an anachronism from an unfortunate past. What if the mainstream media were wrong, just like they have been on nearly all societal issues over the past century? What if men, playing their Godly roles, were a necessity for a healthy culture and community? What if the cultural and moral degradation we witness all around us today began when men retreated years ago from the duty owed to wives, families, and communities? What if a group of men, ignoring the carping of numerous critics, assumed the role assigned to them and provided structure and security in the family by being the husband, father and leader needed in today's distressing times? For the last eighteen years of our business we have had front row seats, in living rooms across America and Canada, experiencing first hand the effects of men not assuming their responsibilities.

It wasn't always this way. Duty, a word in ill repute today, meant something to the men of the past. Character, honor, fidelity, all words laughed at today, were, in the past, concepts worthy of sacrifice. Men believed that life without character, honor, and duty, was dissolute and hardly worth living. Many examples of duty and honor come to mind, but let us share the history of two men who had conviction and were willing to sacrifice for what they believed. Both lived in England during stormy religious times with Catholics against Anglicans against Puritans, each seeking to learn and live truth in an age where truth still mattered. In an era before religious freedoms, it's easy for us moderns to judge critically the behaviors of all three denominations. But it's important to remember it was the struggles of these three groups that produced the religious, political, and spiritual freedoms enjoyed by the colonial Americans, and through them, enjoyed by us today. It's important, when studying history, to place one-self in the culture of the times, studying the courage and convictions based upon the culture as it was then, not as it is now.

Hugh Latimer and Nicholas Ridley, both preachers and teachers, were each sentenced to burn for their religious positions. The easy way out of the dilemma would have been to recant, but both Latimer and Ridley were convinced by scripture and reason, that to save themselves, they would be rejecting God and God's Word. The two men were therefore tied to opposite sides of a wooden stake. The executioners stacked wood under their feet, preparing to set the whole on fire. At that point Ridley started to falter, losing his composure under the immense pressure, but Latimer, in a calm assuring tone, said to his friend, "Be of good comfort, Master Ridley, and play the man; we shall this day light such a candle, by God's grace, in England, as I trust shall never be put out." The deaths of Latimer, Ridley, and another man named Cranmer (the three men becoming known as the 'Oxford Martyrs'), are still commemorated in Oxford to this day by the Victorian Martyrs' Memorial near the site of their execution.

When we think of the great sacrifices such men of conviction have made to build the foundation of the privileges and rights we enjoy today, we are moved with respect and awe. It makes one wonder where the men of today are who will "play the man."

We can consider this particularly in the realm of marriage. It takes two people to make one good marriage, but if the marriage is struggling, men should ensure they've done everything within their power to make things right. How many times have we seen a crushed wife crying over a man-child in the role of her husband — a man in body, but a child in responsibilities – wondering if he would ever grow into the man he was called to be? How many times have we witnessed a woman reading her tenth book on marriage relationships while the first one lies unread by the man's bedside? Men who in former times likely would have sacrificed their time, money, and lives to protect their families, today seemingly cannot find the courage within to even read one book with the goal of protecting and enhancing their marriage. The words in the marriage covenant "for better or worse" now mean "for better or else" to many men. Husbands, it's time for you to play the man.

One article recently posed the question: Where have all the fathers gone? Absentee fathers have created an incalculable loss in millions of young boys' and girls' lives, who are growing up without the reassuring protection and leadership of their father. Just a cursory look at the data tells the heartbreaking story of radical increases in teenage dropouts, crimes, pregnancies, and suicides. Mainstream media loves to call the tune, but conveniently isn't around when it's time to pay the piper. The men, women, and children are charged with paying the bill, suffering the pain associated with the fractured relationships, while the media runs off on its next social experiment. We can criticize 19th century North America, mocking their social conservatism, finding fault with their quaint customs, but when looking in the eyes of a deserted wife left with young children, the denigration of the older way has a hollow ring. It's time every father steps up to the plate and learns how to lovingly serve his wife and nurture his children while providing a disciplined home environment. Young boys need to know they have what it takes to be men. Young girls need to know their father loves them and is willing to protect them against anyone who threatens his princess, until such a time a young prince comes along to defend her honor in his stead. This is just one of the many roles of the father, a role that is practically lost today, causing immeasurable harm to so many young men and women. If you are a father, it's time for you to play the man.

A popular book recently asked the question: Where have all the leaders gone? So many men, checked out of their marriages, checked out on their children, complete the dismal Triple Crown by also checking out of leadership. You cannot be a bum in one area of your life while being a star in another. Either leadership will grow all areas or lack of leadership will stunt them. Men must lead their homes, learning the principles of leadership necessary to serve within society. Because of our warped understanding of leadership, many assume leadership means dictatorship, but nothing could be further from the truth. Leadership is based upon servanthood and a willingness to serve others. When a man gets the leadership right in his home, he can then step forward to lead in his community, having the confidence engendered by a stable home.

> Leadership is based upon servanthood and a willingness to serve others.

In order to have men lead in the homes and society we must raise up a group of leaders who accept responsibility. As C. S. Lewis wrote in his classic *Men Without Chests*, "We make men without chests and expect of them virtue and enterprise. We laugh at honor and are shocked to find traitors in our midst. We castrate and bid the geldings be fruitful."

A vital part in the resurgence of North America is the restoration of manhood, ending the self-inflicted castration of the male. True servant leadership based upon character, courage, and convictions, is still alive in a remnant of men. This remnant has hibernated long enough. We can no longer remain inactive. We can no longer allow our wives and children to be damaged by our lack of leadership. We can no longer pass the buck. It's time to step up to the plate. Just as Latimer encouraged Ridley, allow us to encourage you, "Be of good comfort, North American males, and play the man; we shall light such a candle, by God's grace, as we trust shall never be put out." **Play the man!**

"A person who always looks inside, cannot serve others outside. A person who never looks inside is dangerous to the outside world. Success is an inside then outside assignment."

Oh, if we could only find a government official who would spend his own money and sleep with his own wife.

Many people are more enamored with their credit-based lifestyle than with true wealth creation.

"Treat your business like a game. Define the game, keep score and win."

"Leaders should not avoid challenges but display their leadership by solving them."

Solitude in proper doses does wonders for the soul.

You can learn a lot about people when you discover what motivates them.

157

"The mantra of winners everywhere: take action now!"

"A leader doesn't need all the answers, but he does need character and hunger."

"It is much easier to talk about leadership to people than it is to truly lead people."

"In leadership, 99 percent belief is 100 percent unbelief. Doubt is its biggest enemy."

"There is just something inspiring about a person who will get back up and try again."

"A person will likely be defined by a few pivotal decisions in his or her life."

"People will never follow someone they do not trust. Never sacrifice your character to impress others."

"There will come a time when you will have to explain your actions."

"Leaders still get butterflies. The difference is that they have learned to help them fly in formation."

"It won't be One World Order, it will be One World Order you around."

"You have to convince yourself you are worthy of achieving that vision you see in your mind's eye."

"Leaders cannot remain silent in the face of injustice."

"Elections have consequences."

"Just as a gardener pulls weeds from a garden, leaders pull weeds from their thinking before they spread."

"One of life's greatest blessings is discovering one's purpose and working in that direction with all one's might."

THE BEST LEADERS HAVE FUN

"It's kind of fun to do the impossible," said Walt Disney.

"People rarely succeed unless they have fun in what they are doing," wrote Dale Carnegie.

"I never did a day's work in my life. It was all fun," said Thomas Edison.

"If you watch a game, it's fun. If you play it, it's recreation. If you work at it, it's golf," quipped Bob Hope.

And finally, "Girls just want to have fun," or so says the popular song. (There is at least some justification for the suspicion that the proverbial jury is still out on this one.)

This concept of fun seems prevalent in our thoughts and speech. Everyone seems to have some sort of attachment to it, some philosophy about it, and some amount of understanding of the term. We "make fun," "have fun," and are sometimes called "fun." But just what is this word all about? Could it be any fun at all to explore the various facets of fun itself?

Economists (who by reputation are likely far from experts on the subject) might be inclined to call "fun" a "good." This is not a value judgment, as comparing something to "bad," but rather a term meant to describe the means to satisfy man's wants. Goods are anything that bring about satisfaction to the economic actor, or desirous man. See, it's just no fun from this angle.

So let's try another. Bohemians are famous for their worship of this word "fun," or rather, its realization in their lives. They chase it, pursue it, covet it, cherish it, and continually and shamelessly idolize it.

Then there are the legalistic whose highest value appears to be the absence of fun, or the non-fun, or the anti-fun. They've missed grace and found rules. Crinkled brows and stern faces seem to indicate that fun is bad mostly because it appears to be fun. (Do not be offended. This is all in fun.)

So some people worship fun while others prohibit it. Yet Disney, Carnegie, and Edison all seem to indicate that fun itself is a factor in productive living. Each of us, no doubt, carry fond memories of fun moments and fun times with fun people. In short, it's fun to have fun (at which point the reader must feel we have arrived at no very great distance from where we started!)

Allow us to posit that fun is the by-product of a number of other correct factors all being in place at the same time.

To illustrate this idea, let's consider the negative. It is nearly impossible to "have fun" when something important is amiss in our lives. We cannot sincerely laugh and worry at the same time. We cannot really have fun while grieving, regretting, or hurting. Fun, then, won't alight in our lives unless the conditions are correct. It is at this point we might enjoy looking at the official definition (taken from Webster's, definition #2):

FUN: A MOOD FOR FINDING OR MAKING AMUSEMENT.

Aha! It's a mood! Well that explains a lot! Our moods come and go, change and morph, in reaction to our environment, circumstances, and how we choose to perceive and react to those stimuli. So fun, in the manner in which we are considering it, is an enjoyable mood that amuses us.

So why have we ventured this far along what feels to be a philosophical journey, and a rather obvious one, at that? Simply to realize that fun is a mood to be induced under the correct conditions. And why is this helpful? Because, in such a light, fun can be seen as a tool. Say what?

Yes, a tool. Fun is a condition, and according to Disney, Carnegie, and Edison at least, a productive one, in which people are amused, entertained, and for which they are grateful. In other words, it is a blessing in their lives. What better tool could the would-be leader learn about and learn to utilize than one that blesses, enriches, entertains, and leads to productivity? And this (don't miss it) is the point of this meandering discussion: the best leaders understand how to have fun and how to invoke fun in the lives of their followers. The best leaders know when to lighten the mood, how to arrange circumstances in a way that is likely to produce fun, and how to make the shared tasks of their teams enjoyable. This accomplishes several things:

1. Better mental health of the participants
2. A shared sense of mirth (and therefore belonging)
3. A lack of heaviness which leads to bad attitudes and negative outlooks
4. A relief of tension which prohibits productive action and creative thinking
5. Less relational problems, which result from too much seriousness or overblown perspectives on self-importance
6. Quicker passing of time for more menial tasks
7. Makes further work more attractive and minimizes "project dread"

We have witnessed leaders who understood the power of fun injected into situations at just the right time. Tense moments were diffused, heaviness was lifted, and optimism was restored through simple gestures of fun. Other leaders have established fun as a pervasive element in their very corporate culture. (Southwest Airlines and Zappos come to mind.) The very best of leaders understand that working in the area of one's natural gifts is often the most fun work that exists for that individual, and ultimately, it is to this that the quotes at the beginning of this article were alluding. When we are doing what we are built to do, called to do, and deeply motivated to do, we will enjoy it. We will have fun. Therefore, as author and researcher Jim Collins put it, the best leaders will make sure their people are "in the correct seats on the bus." However, it will often take a lot of work (that may not be much fun) to get to the point where the organization is correctly arranged and people have earned their way into positions of their gifting. Learning, striving, and climbing are often arduous and difficult activities. It is through these stretches that the best leaders interject doses of fun along the way. Fun thus becomes like grease in a machine – it carries away heat and chips and minimizes friction.

Obviously, moderation is the key. Neither the Bohemians nor the legalists have it right. But properly utilized, fun can be a very effective implement in the leader's toolbox. It will lead to greater productivity by happier people.

To close, let's consider two more comments regarding this topic of fun.

"I cannot even imagine where I'd be today were it not for that handful of friends who have given me a heart full of joy. Let's face it, friends make life a lot more fun." – Charles Swindoll

"Skiing combines outdoor fun with knocking down trees with your face." – Dave Barry

"I can tell more about a leader by spending an hour with his team than I can by spending an hour with him – Culture matters."

"Learn, Do, Teach is the cycle of a leader's life."

ONE PERSON CAN MAKE A DIFFERENCE.

THINGS ARE RARELY AS BAD AS THEY SEEM; USUALLY A BETTER PERSPECTIVE OR SMALL PIECE OF NEW EVIDENCE IS ALL THAT'S NEEDED TO RESTORE FAITH.

"Anyone can throw money at a problem, but leaders develop creative solutions. Think more, spend less, win bigger."

"If you climb to the top of the mountain, you cannot expect others to see what you see."

THERE IS ALMOST NOTHING WORTHWHILE A PERSON CAN DO THAT WON'T BE OBSTINATELY OPPOSED BY SOMEONE.

CRITICS ARE SPECTATORS.

162

"Most are playing it safe in life, even though none of us is getting out alive."

"A group's leadership limit is reached when voluntarism ends and compulsion begins."

66It is not what happens to you in life, but how you think about what happens to you in life that matters most.99

66It's time to start believing you can accomplish anything your dreams suggest.99

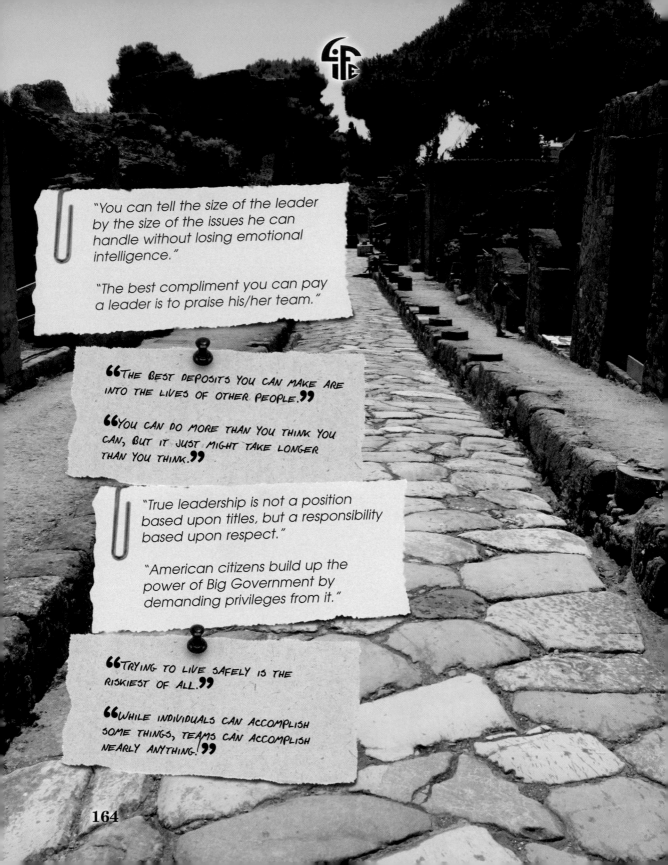

"You can tell the size of the leader by the size of the issues he can handle without losing emotional intelligence."

"The best compliment you can pay a leader is to praise his/her team."

"The best deposits you can make are into the lives of other people."

"You can do more than you think you can, but it just might take longer than you think."

"True leadership is not a position based upon titles, but a responsibility based upon respect."

"American citizens build up the power of Big Government by demanding privileges from it."

"Trying to live safely is the riskiest of all."

"While individuals can accomplish some things, teams can accomplish nearly anything."

Response Ability

Being responsible means we are response-able. Between stimulus and response, we humans have the power to choose. This is what separates us from mere animals who rely solely upon instinct. Thank you to Stephen Covey for this insight.

Acknowledging this, then, we must take stock of our Response Ability. How well do we do responding to the obstacles of life? How effective are we in our responses? Are they measured, correct, and appropriate? Are they productive and emotionally sound?

Far too many people react emotionally, childishly, rashly, and recklessly to the things that happen in their lives. Strangely, I contend they actually enjoy it! I observed a thirty-something man on a cell phone in a public restroom yesterday berate someone while watching himself in the mirror. The only thing more ridiculous than what he was saying was how he was saying it. He seemed to be getting some kind of satisfaction from playing the idiot.

Don't be like him. Stay away from antics and the instinctive responses that should be left to animals. Be an emotionally mature human being, with love in your heart, understanding in your voice, and resolution in your attitude. Remember that no matter what happens to you, it is within your freedom of choice to respond appropriately. Choose. And choose wisely.

> *Between stimulus and response, we humans have the power to choose.*

HOW HIGH IS YOUR RESPONSE ABILITY?

"You cannot seize your future until you let go of your past."

"Leaders look for reasons to win while others look for reasons to quit."

"Most people will sacrifice truth for promotion while a few will sacrifice promotion for truth."

"The masses are motivated by self-interest, but demagogues know that hatred is stronger than self-interest."

A GOOD BOOK IS HARD TO FINISH BECAUSE IT CONTINUALLY MAKES ONE PUT IT DOWN AND TAKE ACTION!

THE SAME VIRTUES THAT MADE AMERICA FREE WILL BE REQUIRED TO KEEP IT FREE.

"Why is it that people who seem to know so much do so little?"

"Grace is unmerited forgiveness received by repentance. Don't disgrace grace by not forgiving others who truly repent."

BEWARE OF ANYONE TOO SURE OF HOW THE WORLD WORKS.

LEADERSHIP IS AN ART PERFORMED BY IMPERFECT PEOPLE LEADING OTHER IMPERFECT PEOPLE INTO AN IMPERFECT FUTURE NONE OF THEM HAS YET SEEN.

Destiny Restored from Above

Shattered by broken decisions,
Trusting in man no more,
People perish through lack of vision,
My heart is broken to the core.

Honor and character viciously assailed,
Faith cast to the ground,
My courage & strength nearly failed,
I am lost, groping to be found.

I stared into the dark abyss,
Searching for relief,
Finding nothing but hopelessness,
In my doubting unbelief.

Perplexed without a clue,
Burdened by my loss,
One answer rings tried and true,
The Son of Man on the cross.

Lost and infected with sin's disease,
Satan mocking me blow after blow,
I surrender self upon my knees,
Feel Jesus' blood begin to flow.

Blinded by His light,
His glory powerfully revealed,
Death conquered by His might,
God's plan mercifully unsealed.

Good overcomes evil in a fight,
Nobodies to somebodies in His love,
Jesus Christ, what a precious sight,
My destiny restored from above.

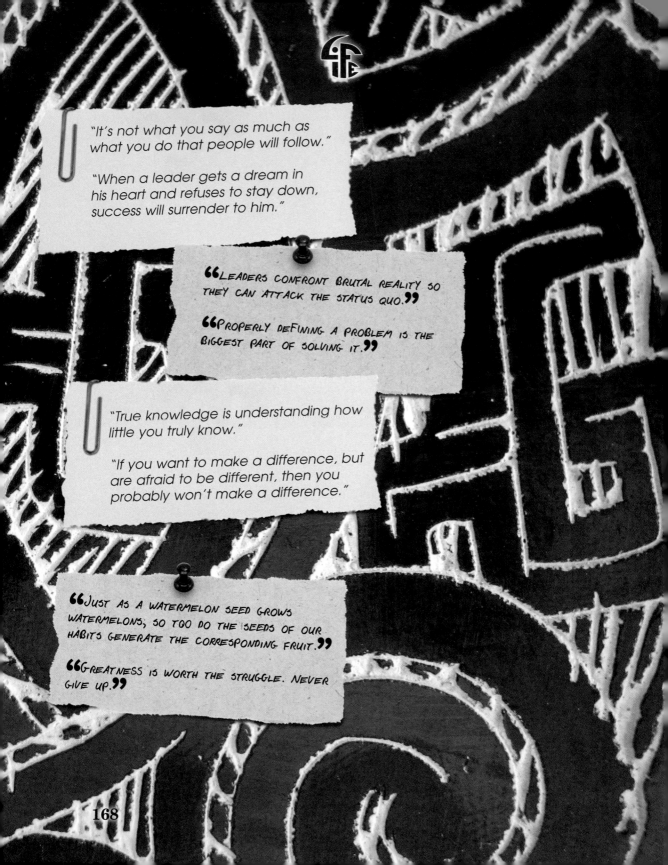

"It's not what you say as much as what you do that people will follow."

"When a leader gets a dream in his heart and refuses to stay down, success will surrender to him."

"Leaders confront brutal reality so they can attack the status quo."

"Properly defining a problem is the biggest part of solving it."

"True knowledge is understanding how little you truly know."

"If you want to make a difference, but are afraid to be different, then you probably won't make a difference."

"Just as a watermelon seed grows watermelons, so too do the seeds of our habits generate the corresponding fruit."

"Greatness is worth the struggle. Never give up."

It's Not That Simple

Asking good questions of yourself is one key to coming up with good answers. One such question ought to be: How can I make this simpler?

One of the easiest things to do in anything is to add complication. We complicate our tasks, our lives, our jobs, and our relationships. We seem to be masters of adding: we add responsibility, workload, possessions, stress, and strain to our days. We add features to our equipment, modifications to our toys, and events to our calendars. It seems the answer to any question always involves more.

But what if it didn't?

What if the answer to the better questions involved less?

What if the big breakthrough in your business, career, or whatever resided in your ability to make what you are doing simpler?

What if you could prune, condense, and simplify?

What if you could make things easier and more straightforward?

Anyone can add; it takes courage to subtract.

> Asking good questions of yourself is one key to coming up with good answers.

SO GET THINKING: THINK ABOUT LESS, EASIER, AND SIMPLER; AND TRUST US, DOING SO IS NOT THAT EASY OR SIMPLE.

You Told Me
Otherwise

I thought her a beauty
And took to her smile,
But you told me otherwise
Suspecting her guile.

I liked his stories
And thought them a laugh,
But you told me otherwise
Said don't believe half.

Their group took me in
And made me feel part,
But you told me otherwise
And picked them apart.

I wonder how life
Feels walked in your shoes,
Where nobody's good enough
And none you'll approve.

It's good that you're there
To show other's flaws,
I'd probably think them fine
If you caused no pause.

But you make me think
How sad it must be,
To see mere scary water
When watching the sea.

You told me of you
And wanted my praise,
But you told me otherwise
In living these ways.

❝Be willing to give up what you want in the here and now for what you really want long term.❞

❝Life has no rewind and it's time to act like it.❞

"Lazy leaders throw money at problems, but successful leaders apply better thinking to them."

"The winds of change can be used like a kite to lift you higher or like a tumbleweed to toss you about."

❝The battle in the trenches of our habits is where success is won or lost.❞

❝Most people have a point at which their pragmatism overcomes their principles.❞

"Your business is going to change, either led by you or your competitors."

"Leaders must lead people & manage the numbers, but most manage people & damage the numbers."

171

"Leadership is most needed on the front lines, not the backrooms."

"The greatest way for leaders to receive more responsibilities is to prove faithful in their current ones."

❝Leaders are dealers in perspective. When in a crisis, leaders keep their heads because they keep things in perspective.❞

❝The pursuit of significance and service is the surest route to happiness.❞

"The more I study the habits of the successful and unsuccessful, the more I am convinced that success isn't an accident."

"Don't let the things that are outside of your control stop you from doing the things that you can control."

❝Justification is the enabler of cowardice. People are capable of abominable acts as long as they can justify it to themselves.❞

❝Freedom is a child of responsibility.❞

Friendship

There are thousands of books on money, business, marriage, child rearing, diet, exercise, cooking, and gardening. Strangely, however, is the relative scarcity of those on the subject of friendship.

A little over a year ago, my (Chris's) bride underwent brain surgery to remove a large tumor. It was physically traumatic, life threatening, and very scary. Terri emerged from the experience healthy and armed with yet another obvious blessing straight from God. Ordeals such as that demonstrate a lot of things. First, they have a staggering power to realign one's priorities. And secondly, they reveal the real friends in one's life.

There were callers and well-wishers, people sending meals, others sending cards. Several showed up in the waiting room and rode shotgun through the entire day of surgery, some returning the next morning, others staying the night. Terri had a nurse friend assist in the recovery room the first night, and another awaiting her arrival at our house upon her hospital discharge. From the moment she arrived home until several weeks after, Terri received around-the-clock care from an army of girlfriends who had mobilized, scheduled themselves, and swooped onto the scene to nurture, support, administer medication, provide child care, and just "be there."

It was awesome.

It was love in motion.

It was true friendship.

Friendship is hard to define. It has no official commitments like marriage. It has no familial ties like parenthood or relationships with siblings. It carries no consistent definition. But like great art, while defying description, it is readily identifiable when it is experienced.

Terri's surgery was a reminder to us both of the value of true friendships in our life. We treasure the incredible people God has placed around us, and we pray we have been the kind of friends to them they have been to us.

Friendships should never be taken for granted, as they provide grounding, comfort, companionship, depth, meaning, and enjoyment. Give some consideration to the friendships in your life. Nurture them. Invest. Contribute. Serve. Laugh, live, and forge tighter the relationships that truly are one of life's greatest treasures.

"Some people stumble over the truth, pick themselves up, and go on their way as if nothing happened at all."

"Leadership is planned assault on the status quo."

"Greatness isn't for those who dabble, nor for those who deliberate, but for those who decide."

"You can succeed beyond your past, but not beyond your belief."

"Life is about what you give, not what you get!"

"Being counter-cultural and running against the herd takes work, but it is exhilarating."

"What if we demanded the same excellence from ourselves that we demand of our sports heros?"

"This might sound obvious, but one who writes must first have something to say."

"True liberty ensures no one infringes upon your right to be wrong, unless your wrong infringes upon another's liberty."

"We consider to be profound those things that enter our understanding through a window we didn't know we possessed."

"Creativity demands hard work as condition for its release. Then later the laborer is insulted with the word 'talent.'"

"Anyone can start well. It's finishing that counts."

"If you attempt to please everyone all the time, you will not please anyone, including yourself, most of the time."

"When hit with financial challenges many people curl up like a roly-poly bug."

Multum, Non Multa

C. Plinius Caecilius Secundus (61 – 114 A.D.), also known as Pliny the Younger, said *"Multum, Non Multa."* Translated, it says, "Much, not many."

I am not sure what he meant by it or why he said it, after all, I'm no philologist. And, being as he's been dead a long time, I feel quite free in the following interpretation: Quality, not quantity.

Think about how many applications this has to our modern, busy, frenzied, materialistic lives.

As applied to friendships.

As applied to possessions.

As applied to accomplishments.

We trade so much of ourselves for more, more, more, when instead we should likely be demanding better, better, better.

My favorite saying in the movie *Hitch* was: "Life is not the number of breaths you take, it's the moments that take your breath away." Those moments are available to us all. They exist in the gaps between the things we have scheduled, planned, organized, and orchestrated. They occur in and around all the other events we trick ourselves into thinking are important. Suddenly one of those little moments will occur: a hug, a cute question from a child, a warm compliment from a friend, an act of kindness from a stranger, a look of honesty from an acquaintance, and like hearing an old song, we remember.

Let us not be so consumed with getting through that we let it all pass by.

Let us not be in such a hurry to get there that we don't experience what's here.

Let us not be so obsessed with making a living that we miss out on making a life.

Much, not many.

"Truth is sweet to the ears, but painful to the heart until you live by it."

Human wisdom leads to pride, but Godly wisdom leads to humility."

Remember: Your customers actually want to be amazed. They stand at the ready to brag about you!

OK. I get it that we are here to serve others. But what are they here for?

"An honest government should be less the voice of the people & more the voice of justice."

"Listen Up: Leadership at the highest levels has more to do with listening than speaking."

Learning is so much fun, I wonder how they managed to make it NOT SO during my formal schooling years?

I've seen people get such long faces it would take two barbers to shave them.

Don't Just Tell Them — Tell Them A Story

Color movies were instantly more popular than the previous black and white variety. Children resist direct instruction, but *ask* for stories to be told to them. We remember what we see much better than what we merely hear. All these and more speak to the fact that communication is almost always best when aligned with the natural human tendency to think and learn in terms of stories.

Stories are more than just mere entertainment — they are the language of the imagination.

So don't be so quick to rush out your facts and figures, keep your platitudes and preachments in the holster, and quit with your pronouncements and proclamations. If you truly want to communicate, whether to a large audience or small, formally or informally, through the written word or spoken, you must realize the importance of creating a picture in the mind's eye(s) of your listener(s).

Example: When I was but a wee engineer just cutting my teeth in the profession, I had the good fortune to be thrown in with several elderly gentlemen who were extremely accomplished in the field. These guys were so good at technical things they actually conducted races to see who could solve complex puzzles and riddles the most quickly. I was eager to learn all I could from such a wealth of experience all around me. Unfortunately, much of that wealth was inaccessible to me because I could never seem to catch much of what these men so casually reported. As a case in point, there was a discussion one day in a meeting in which I asked a question of one of these men. I was simply inquiring for a restatement of his conclusion to a complicated set of data he had presented – something along the lines of, "So would it be better to use copper or magnesium for this application?" I will never forget the reply. It wasn't, "copper." It wasn't, "magnesium." Nor was it "both," or "neither." Instead I was answered with something like this: "Well, if you look at the second column, copper is 67.98 and magnesium is 56.37." The reason his answer failed to answer, so to speak, was he was forcing me to construct my own picture from data that, although apparently clear and meaningful to him, was nothing more than numbers to me. I had no context in which to understand the meaning or magnitude of his numerical findings. In short, what I needed for him to do was paint me the picture, not give me the dimensions of the frame.

In the above paragraph, what have I done? I have given an illustration that (hopefully) demonstrates my point – the best communication is done through illustrations!

Communicate through stories. Bring your points to life with illustrations. Give examples wherever possible. Come up with analogies and similes and metaphors. I learned in a book by Stuart Olyott that the best preachers first state their message, then illustrate it, and then apply it practically to their listeners' lives. This is sage advice, not only for preachers, but also for everyone who wishes to communicate more effectively. Otherwise, all of your knowledge and preparation and results and platitudes and conclusions will hardly even be heard – much less understood or long remembered.

Bring your points to life with illustrations.

"ONE THING THE ONE WORLD GOVERNMENT WACKOS PROBABLY HAVEN'T CONSIDERED IS HOW BORING THAT WOULD MAKE THE OLYMPICS."

"CROWDS ARE PREDICTABLE BUT INDIVIDUALS ARE MUCH LESS SO. THEORISTS, ECONOMISTS, SOCIOLOGISTS BEWARE."

"Our government no longer serves the original USA, but instead serves the United Statists of America."

"Two wrongs don't make a right so don't deceive yourself by pointing to others' faults to forgive your poor behavior."

"SUNSHINE IS GREAT. I REALLY DO THINK I'M SOLAR POWERED. I WONDER IF I CAN GET CARBON CREDITS FOR THAT?"

"A BIG PART OF LEADING IS TEACHING."

"Be not elated by fortune, nor depressed by adversity. – Every great leader must have emotional control to rise above the situation."

"All your weaknesses are just stepping stones to future strengths."

Leaders as Service Revolvers

A farmer ambled along the lonely country road heading to his humble farm one dusk evening when he dozed off and ran off the road. Ditches were deep in those parts, and his overloaded pickup truck sank far into the muddy crevice and came to rest on its side. Unfortunately, the farmer had been hauling both a pig and a cow in the back. Both were trapped under the truck and wailing in pain. Moments later a state trooper happened by and spotted the truck's headlights pointing oddly along the length of the ditch. Stepping from his cruiser to investigate, the trooper heard the squeals of the dying livestock. Being the merciful sort, the trooper drew his service revolver and fired a shot into the head of the suffering cow, killing him instantly. The pig wailed even louder. In a moment the trooper likewise relieved him of his misery. At this time, the farmer recovered from his unconsciousness and began attempting to free himself from the cab of the crumpled truck. The commotion caught the attention of the trooper who asked, "Are you injured?" To which the farmer replied, "Nope, never felt better in my life!!!!"

Sometimes serving means different things to different parties. In the case of the "service revolver" in the above story, it was an instrument of mercy for the animals, danger for the farmer. Likewise is our leadership in the lives of those we affect. We may have tendencies and strengths that are effective for some, detrimental to others. This is where the best leaders understand that the most impactful leadership often involves treating people uniquely as individuals.

I know in my own leadership experience I find myself "going gentle" with some while "hitting hard" with others. This is because each of us is a uniquely created and infinitely complex individual. We are made in the image of God with special characteristics, abilities, gifts, and tendencies. I can only hope I've gotten the "touch" of such individualized treatment correct!

However, there is a simpler lesson to be gained from the farmer and the trooper, and that is one of service. The trooper was trying to help. He saw a need and did his duty. This, too, is illustrative of the proper function of a leader. Leaders serve. Leaders are not meant to sit in a position of authority and soak up the benefits of title. They serve again and again from different positions and in various circumstances. In fact, leaders themselves could be said to be "service revolvers:" going from person to person and from opportunity to opportunity to "be of" service. Their privileges are not for their pleasure but rather for their purpose.

The purpose of a leader is a multi-faceted consideration, including casting and pursuing a vision, service to others, sacrificing self for larger issues, standing in the gap where others fail to stand, holding strong to principles, fighting for causes, taking responsibility, giving credit, eliminating obstacles, developing more leaders, and empowering and encouraging others. Orchestrations, administration, management, and coordination must also be looked to; usually by placing others with requisite gifts into correct positions. In short, leadership is the giving of what you have to others so they can collectively give (and accomplish) more than otherwise would have been possible. We add when we *do*, but we multiply when we *lead*.

Consider your gifts, your position, your abilities, and your blessings. Mobilize those assets in the service of others wherever you are, whoever you are, and with whatever you have, whenever you can.

IN THIS WAY, YOU'LL BE LEADING; YOU'LL BE A SERVICE REVOLVER. JUST DON'T SHOOT ANY FARMERS.

"Writing a book is like writing a letter to all your friends, both current and future."

"Don't tell me about your fears, tell me about your dreams. Set your soul on fire with your life's purpose and the fears will be rolled over."

66INSPIRATION: THE IMPULSE OF CONVICTION AT A KEY MOMENT, REPRESENTATIVE OF WHO ONE TRULY IS IN ALL OTHER MOMENTS.99

66MARRIAGE: WHERE TWO PEOPLE PROMISE TO STICK TOGETHER IN THICKNESS AND HEALTH.99

"What would you dream if you knew you couldn't fail? It takes just as much effort to pursue a small dream as a big dream."

"Sometimes you need to take a step backwards to move three steps forward."

66THE SELFISH LIFE IS NOT WORTH LIVING. FOR THAT MATTER, THE SHELLFISH LIFE IS NOT WORTH LIVING, EITHER.99

66CARING IS FUNDAMENTAL TO LEADERSHIP.99

"You cannot be honest with others until you stop deceiving yourself."

"You can be on the right track and still get run over if you're not moving."

The best leaders build an edifice out of their lives, adding daily to previous accomplishments.

The door to the room of success swings on the hinges of opposition.

"You may lack money, time, contacts, and knowledge, but all of that can be overcome with hunger."

"Leaders make decisions and then make their decisions right through effort."

We don't always get what we want, and we don't always get what we deserve (at least in this life); but we do tend to get what we picture.

185

"You are not free when someone can bend your will through threats of force, but not force of reason."

"Life is a series of mountain climbs; the key is to never get too comfortable at base camp."

"The most boring person to hang around is the one who believes he or she is finished."

"Education does not mean knowing how to read, but being able to discern what is worth reading."

"Never in the history of ideas have so many, known so little, for so long."

"What is greatness worth without a corresponding goodness?"

"Ultimately, your money should work for you, you should not work for it."

"The more you get interested in others, the more you'll discover about this world and the better you'll understand yourself."

"TRAVEL YOUR JOURNEY TO SUCCESS AS A STUDENT AND NOT A CYNIC."

"ONE OF THE MOST ENTERTAINING OF HUMAN BEHAVIORS IS PASSIONATE IGNORANCE."

"Don't envy others' gifts, but do partner with them."

"Reality Check: Life is never as good as it seems at its best and never as bad as it seems at its worst."

"POETS HAVE A KNACK FOR MAKING THINGS SEEM MORE BEAUTIFUL THAN THEY ACTUALLY ARE."

"WE SHOULD TAKE EVERYTHING SERIOUSLY BUT OURSELVES."

"I fear insignificance more than I fear failure."

"You can either learn from mistakes or make excuses for mistakes but you can't do both."

Answering Liberty's Distress Signal

LIFE is a movement of entrepreneurs dedicated to raising the bar on themselves and their communities for life. Consistent success is never achieved without a goal of excellence. Often, people choose pleasing means and then accept whatever results come. But winners choose pleasing results and accept whatever means are necessary to achieve it. Winning is for the few, but anyone can choose to be a part of that few – the few who will do what it takes to win – the few who choose to make a difference.

Today's society stands at a crossroads. People realize that the corporate world is not the "cradle-to-grave" guarantee it was in the decades following World War II; however, so many have been trained only to work for someone else, focusing on security and not opportunity. What happens to a society in which a high percentage of people have been trained to seek a "secure job," but few such jobs are available? Society runs to Big Brother government, seeking the security that government cannot provide. History is filled with examples of governments stifling the entrepreneurial spirit, choking the productive engine of a society's advancement, and sounding the death knell of numerous civilizations, in an attempt to "help the helpless" citizens. North America stands at a crossroads where it either runs to more and more government, (and in the process surrenders its freedom and future,) or returns to its roots, providing freedom and justice for any dreamer who chooses to prosper.

It's time to send a wake up call to the entrepreneurial spirits across North America.

Where are the entrepreneurs, the leaders, and the dreamers who will step to the plate and swing for the fences – win or lose? The time for talking is over and the time for action is upon us. These are historic times with historic ramifications. Just as the founding fathers did in the 18th century, let's pledge our fortunes, our lives, and our sacred honor in this noble cause to restore the American Dream. Liberty has sent out its distress signal. Let's answer the call and be the spark that sets ablaze a new movement for freedom and justice.

"What is the difference between Tact & Politically Correct? Tact is the ability to speak truth in love. Politically Correct surrenders principles for peace."

"Tragedy plus time equals humor. Learn to laugh if you plan to last."

"REAL LEADERS HAVE INFLUENCE BECAUSE THEY HAVE CHARACTER, GET RESULTS, SHARE THE CREDIT AND ACCEPT THE BLAME."

"REAL LEADERS HAVE INFLUENCE BECAUSE OTHERS BELIEVE IN THEIR CAUSE."

"It's easy to be positive when all is positive, but you know you're positive when everything is negative & you are still positive."

"Speak and deal in the Truth – Deluders are deluded by their own delusions."

"STRONG RELATIONSHIPS MAKE FOR STRONG ORGANIZATIONS."

"NEVER FORGET THAT EVERYONE HAS SOMETHING TO OFFER. SOME JUST NEED TO HAVE IT COAXED TO THE SURFACE."

189

"Free Enterprise is the consistent application of freedom applied to the marketplace."

"Anyone can begin a journey of a thousand miles, but only those with persistence finish the journey."

I DON'T SUFFER FOOLS; I ENJOY THEM.

I OFFERED YOU A PENNY FOR YOUR THOUGHTS. I DIDN'T ASK FOR YOUR TWO CENTS WORTH.

"I would rather dream and fail than fail to dream, because I learn lessons in my failures that propel me to victory."

"Big Government Corporatism – A program where all elect the powerful to benefit the few at the expense of the many."

VERY LITTLE THAT IS WORTHWHILE CAN BE ACCOMPLISHED WITHOUT THE COOPERATION OF OTHERS.

TURN YOUR EXCUSES WHY YOU CAN'T INTO REASONS WHY YOU SHOULD!

190

orrinwoodwardblog.com

Orrin Woodward co-wrote the *New York Times* bestsellers *LeaderShift* and *Launching a Leadership Revolution* and has written several other acclaimed books on leadership, including *RESOLVED: 13 Resolutions for LIFE*, which was named as an All-Time Top 100 Leadership Book. He speaks on leadership and personal growth across the globe. His leadership blog has received international acclaim as one of HR's Top 100 Blogs for Management and Leadership and one of Universities Online Top 100 Leadership Blogs.

www.orrinwoodward.com
twitter.com/Orrin_Woodward

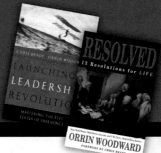

Here is a sample of what the readers in Orrin Woodward's blogging community are saying:

"Orrin, thanks for a great lesson!..." -Matt

"This post reminds me of two things: first, your commitment to God, and second, your unwavering commitment to leadership..." -Brian and Sherry

"...Orrin, each day you help us to understand more of your thinking and also help us to understand ourselves better..." -Ben

"...I read your blog every day...Thank you for your encouraging words every day; they mean so much to me. As I go about my day, I often think to myself...what would Orrin do?..." -Ally

"Another great post - I don't know how you do it, but you just keep coming up with more and more great articles that get the wheels turning in my head!..." -Ann